Economic Analysis of Industrial Agglomeration

Jian Wang

Economic Analysis of Industrial Agglomeration

上海交通大學出版社
SHANGHAI JIAO TONG UNIVERSITY PRESS

Springer

Jian Wang
SHU-UTS SILC Business School
Shanghai University
Shanghai
China

ISBN 978-981-10-7436-3 ISBN 978-981-10-7437-0 (eBook)
https://doi.org/10.1007/978-981-10-7437-0

Jointly published with Shanghai Jiao Tong University Press

Library of Congress Control Number: 2017960933

The print edition is not for sale in China Mainland. Customers from China Mainland please order the print book from: Shanghai Jiao Tong University Press.

Printed on acid-free paper

This Springer imprint is published by Springer Nature
The registered company is Springer Nature Singapore Pte Ltd.
The registered company address is: 152 Beach Road, #21-01/04 Gateway East, Singapore 189721, Singapore

Preface

This book investigates the industrial agglomeration and dispersion within a country under trade liberalization and interregional integration by considering both economic forces and geographical elements. First, it provides a detailed explanation of Krugman's new economic geography (NEG) model and reviews the subsequent refinements of the original model from mainly geographical viewpoints. It points out that many existing models are isomorphic and their two-region assumptions seem unrealistic. Second, this book extends Krugman's original model to a two-country and three-region case where the domestic regions are fully asymmetrical in terms of their sizes and accessibilities to global markets. The simulation results show that when international trade liberalization continues but domestic regions remain poorly integrated, the gate region experiences a change from partial to full agglomeration. When the home country is closed to international trade, the decrease in domestic transport costs makes the hinterland more attractive for manufacturing. However, when it is open to global markets, more manufacturing is undertaken in the gate region during the regional integration. Third, to better explain the reality of developing countries, this book presents an analytical model which assumes that unskilled workers are employed in both traditional and manufacturing sectors. The analytical results show that when the international trade cost is very high, the space economy of home country has full agglomeration in its hinterland and then experiences a process of dispersion until an even industrial distribution exists between the gate and hinterland regions. When the home country is open enough to world markets, firms will first concentrate in the hinterland and then gradually move to the gate region until full agglomeration occurs during regional integration. With further regional economic integration, half of the firms will relocate to the hinterland again, with the other half remaining in the gate region.

Furthermore, the regional economy is assumed to have one manufacturing sector and each manufacturing firm has a unit fixed requirement of capital and a marginal input of labor. Even with constant elasticity substitution (CES) utility function, it can be demonstrated that spatial disparity in terms of wage presents an inverted U-shape respect to regional integration. Accordingly, this book empirically investigates the home market effect (HME) in terms of wages in the case of China by using panel data for the period 1980–2012. It is found that the wages in coastal regions are higher than those in the interior, due to the size differences between regions. Additionally, regional inequality in wages between the coastal and interior regions evolves in an inverted U-shaped curve during periods of regional integration. The evolution of the space economy in China during the past three decades supports the inverted U-shaped pattern predicted by the theoretical models of spatial economics.

By incorporating the geographical elements into the original NEG model, this book explains the increasing industrial agglomeration in countries in the process of international trade liberalization and regional integration. Additionally, the analytical model provides a reasonable explanation for industrial dispersion. Furthermore, it is also successful in explaining that where the agglomeration arises, in addition to providing the rationales for the occurrence of industrial agglomeration. Based on these results, this book suggests that NEG models should incorporate the geographical elements to better explain the reality of developing countries. Moreover, the conclusion about industrial redispersion implies that further improvements of infrastructure between domestic regions represent a feasible way to alleviate the increasing trend of excessive industrial agglomeration.

Shanghai, China Jian Wang

Acknowledgements

This book contains the results of research undertaken at Ritsumeikan University and Shanghai University. The main work is established on the basis of my four published papers over the period from October 2010 to December 2015 (Wang and Zheng, 2012; Wang and Zheng, 2013a; Wang and Zheng, 2013b; Wang and Xu, 2015). I have incurred many intellectual debts during creation of this book. Foremost, I would like to express my sincere gratitude to my supervisor Prof. Xiao-Ping Zheng for the continuous support of my Ph.D. study and research at Ritsumeikan University. He gave me so much inspiration and encouragement during the book writing and the whole doctoral study. I am grateful to my supervisor for his patience and teaching me the importance of every detail. I am also indebted to my subsupervisors, Profs. Masayuki Okawa and Ryoji Hiraguchi of Ritsumeikan University for their valuable comments on my doctoral dissertation. Thanks also go to Prof. Dao-Zhi Zeng from Tohoku University who offered me tremendous help on NEG models.

In addition to those who contributed their ideas to this book, there was also a broad support network. The financial supports I have from the China Scholarship Council (CSC) and KOKUSAITEKI Research Fund of Ritsumeikan University for their support of the international research activities during my doctoral study in Japan are greatly appreciated. I am grateful for these funding sources that allowed me to pursue my doctoral studies. Thanks also extend to the Natural Science Foundation of China (No.71503161) which gives me financial support when I initiate my research at Shanghai University. Moreover, I would like to acknowledge the SHU-UTS SILC Business School at Shanghai University. My research experience has benefitted greatly from the courses that I took, and international atmosphere the school created. Herein, I am most grateful to my coauthor, Prof. Yiwen Bian and Prof. Kangjuan Lv. They give me great help to launch my research work at Shanghai University.

While pursuing research work is a lonely endeavor, it is also not possible without support and love from many. I owe appreciation to my family. They were always supporting me and encouraging me with their best wishes. These years have been a challenging trip. Since I abruptly transform my academic field from geography to economics, the analytical framework of economics is a totally new concept to me but the charm of economics spurs me forward. Regional and urban economics is an old but active field. It is the one I am willing to spend all my time enriching. Last, this book can also be regarded as a brief summary of my early work and I would like to give it to my newborn son as a gift.

Shanghai, China
September 2017

Jian Wang

Contents

List of Figures

List of Tables

Chapter 1
Introduction

1.1 Background of the Book

The agglomeration of economic activities is a universal phenomenon. There are diverse spatial disparities and concentrations at different geographical scales. It is well known that the northern hemisphere dominates the south in terms of the economic development at the global level. Specifically, in the year 2000, the North American Free Trade Area (NAFTA) produced 35% of the world gross domestic product (GDP), the EU (15 countries) 25%, and East Asia 23%; moreover, this agglomeration of GDP in these three regions has increased in recent years. Regional economic disparity is also reflected in the diversity of regions and cities within a country. The core regions attract most of the population and industries from the periphery, like the Tokyo metropolitan area in Japan and the three metropolitan circles (Yangtze River delta, Pearl River delta, and area surrounding the Bohai Sea) in China. In many countries, there is a specific region that leads the nation in manufacturing activity, job creation, and drawing population from other regions. At a more micro scale, industrial districts as a typical case involving large volume of firms with linkages of information and production, such as the Silicon Valley and Wenzhou industrial clusters in China, demonstrate various types of local specialization. It is observed that peaks and troughs in the spatial distribution of population, wages, and manufacturing are striking features of the real world economy. To some extent, economic activities exist in time and space, and we cannot imagine that spatial element to be absent in the study of economics. Nevertheless, traditional mainstream economics has seldom been concerned with where firm production and household consumption occur. Studies charting the evolution of spatial disparities are always notably ignored, and the research on economic geography at best plays a marginal role in economic theory.

It was not until Paul Krugman's seminal paper "Increasing returns and economic geography" (1991), which used a general equilibrium framework, that microeconomic rationales concerning the occurrence of industrial agglomeration began to

J. Wang, *Economic Analysis of Industrial Agglomeration*,
https://doi.org/10.1007/978-981-10-7437-0_1

emerge. Krugman successfully obtained endogenous agglomeration to explain the economic structure of the core-periphery in a corresponding geographical space. Since then, there have been numerous refinements to this perspective related to investigating the mechanism of economic agglomeration and formation of the core-periphery structure. The main conclusions of these core-periphery models tell us that high transport costs lead to the dispersion of industry into two symmetrical regions and that industrial agglomeration occurs when transport costs are low (Krugman 1991; Ottaviano et al. 2002; Forslid and Ottaviano 2003). The emergence of these studies has accordingly created a new field of economics often referred to as new economic geography (NEG).

With regard to the attention to space in economics research, NEG is obviously not ahead of the game. As antecedents, urban economics and regional science traditionally dealt with the question of how economic activities organize use of space. In particular, urban economics has given valuable insights into land use within a city and the formation of an urban system. On the other hand, regional science offers valuable insights using more rigorous models (Fujita et al. 1999, p. 25). However, leaving aside other shortcomings, the core weakness of urban economics and regional science is that they deal with agglomeration as a black box where they assume that economies of agglomeration bring about economic agglomeration. Unlike its antecedents, therefore, NEG attempts to enter the black box of agglomeration economies and show the self-reinforcing character of spatial concentration using more fundamental considerations (Fujita et al. 1999, p. 4).

NEG is successful in explaining the riddle of spatial disparity and the cluster of economic activities in geographical space. The story of economic agglomeration is represented as the outcome of the interaction between centripetal forces that pull economic activities together and centrifugal forces that separate them. In addition, the mechanism of the model is explicitly derived based on a full microeconomic foundation. The modeling tricks of NEG succeed in synthesizing increasing returns, monopolistic competition, transport costs, and evolution dynamics in a reasonable way. Thus, NEG is also regarded as the fourth wave of the increasing-returns revolution in economics in the last decades.[1]

Admittedly, NEG models precisely investigate the nature of pecuniary externalities and help us to understand the origins of agglomeration forces. To some extent, NEG has reached a certain level of conceptual and theoretical maturity. However, despite its countless refinements and rapid progress following Krugman's seminal paper, NEG still has several deficiencies. First, it is imperative for us to step back and consider what is lacking in the original NEG model. As Behrens et al. (2006a) commented, NEG has allowed us to combine the old ingredients through a new recipe to increase the understanding of economic agglomeration. However, NEG models overemphasize the role of pure economic mechanism in explaining

[1]Since the end of the 1970s, the models of monopolistic competition have become tractable in the presence of increasing returns. It was initially proposed by Dixit and Stiglitz (1977). Then, this framework developed into the engine of theoretical models in various studies and applied in terms of industrial organization, new trade theory, and new growth theory (Fujita et al. 1999, p 3).

the formation of agglomeration and neglect the complexities and difference of natural endowment, such as geographical features in the real world. Although the models are simple and illuminating, they are unable to explain the rich and complex hierarchy that characterizes the space economy (Ottaviano and Thisse 2004). For analytical tractability, in terms of the spatial setup, only a hypothetical and simple two-region economy is assumed.

Second, as economic integration proceeds, the question arises of how the economic landscape will change over time after the core-periphery pattern. We have seen that extreme agglomeration in one region may give rise to various extra costs related to production and living that can trigger a process of industrial dispersion. However, it is fair to say that industrial dispersion still receives little attention. Similarly, there have been no definitive investigations combining geographic features and industrial dispersion to explain the actual industrial location patterns. It is worth noting that although NEG models tell us why agglomeration occurs, they are largely unconcerned with where the agglomeration arises. The early core-periphery model claimed that the decrease in transport costs leads to industrial agglomeration in one of the two regions. In other words, the two homogeneous regions seem to enjoy the same opportunity to become the center. This is obviously inconsistent with the real economic world.

We find that the springboard of NEG has focused entirely on the advanced economies, mainly that of the United States. NEG originally attempted to give a reasonable explanation for the uneven distribution of manufacturing. Today, however, most manufacturing growth takes place in emerging nations. Developing economies, particularly Brazil, Russia, India, China, and South Africa (the BRICS countries), bear the main task of manufacturing production for the world. Within these countries, the economic landscape is reshaped in the process of international trade liberalization and regional integration. Asymmetrical geographical features play an important role in shaping the space economy. Especially in developing countries, the geographic accessibilities and original regional size cannot be assumed to be symmetrical. Moreover, the internal space economy is simultaneously affected by domestic regional integration and globalization. The original two-region model of NEG does not distinguish these symmetrical geographical features.

1.2 Purposes of the Book

Despite the success of NEG theories, we find that some refining of the original NEG model needs to be done to make it closer to the real world. This book has multiple purposes geared toward settling the issues mentioned above. Its first purpose is to provide a detailed review of related literatures after Krugman's core-periphery model (1991) and demonstrate that the most of the existing NEG models are symmetrical in that regions or countries are assumed to have the same sizes and accessibilities to markets, which is not realistic and is unable to explain the real spatial economy. Since several surveys already exist on the review of the development of NEG, this book focuses on the geographical viewpoints and shows that it is important for NEG to take into account the full asymmetry in terms of different regional sizes and accessibilities so that it can adapt its theories to more accurately reflect the real word.

The second purpose of this book is to investigate the impact of international trade liberalization and regional integration on the distribution of industrial activities within countries such as China. The related NEG literature simply emphasizes the economic forces reshaping the space economy, and these are always considered second nature (self-reinforcing economic forces). Evidently, the success of coastal regions in China relative to other regions is accounted for by the interaction of geographical advantage (first nature) and self-reinforcing economic forces (second nature). A similar phenomenon can be witnessed in the border regions of Mexico. The self-reinforcing forces have been extensively studied in recent NEG models. However, the combination of this kind of second nature and the first nature remains to be pursued. How the space economy evolves during regional integration and international liberalization will therefore be investigated here.

The third purpose of this book is to study industrial agglomeration and dispersion using an analytical model. From the early models of NEG, most of the literature relied heavily on the simulation method. The intractability of early studies prevented the spread of NEG and the elucidation of policy implications to some extent. This book will attempt to provide analytical results to explain the industrial dispersion. Moreover, to better explain the reality of developing countries, it is assumed that unskilled workers are employed in both the traditional and manufacturing sectors. In fact, we know from the work of Williamson (1965) and others that the spatial disparities undergo a process from increasing to decreasing. This means that as development proceeds, economic agglomeration spreads from core regions to peripheral ones. This raises the following questions: Is there a normal pattern whereby industrial redispersion occurs during the economic integration? When the regions are asymmetrical in terms of accessibility, what are the industrial location patterns? Do the center regions always dominate the whole economic system? This book takes some steps towards addressing these issues and attempts to give a reasonable explanation for such characteristics.

1.3 Organization of the Book

This book comprises six chapters. This chapter explains the background and purposes of this book. Chapter 2 gives a selective and related literature review of NEG models. It presents the standard seminal core-periphery model (Krugman 1991) more formally and introduces those extensions that step outside the canonical framework. This discussion is mainly concerned with spatial scale from a geographical viewpoint and divides previous works into symmetrical and asymmetrical cases based on how they deal with the accessibility to markets and region sizes.

Chapter 3 extends Krugman's original NEG model to account for a two-country, three-region case where the home country is fully asymmetrical in terms of its size and access to global markets. Under the full asymmetry consideration, the effects of regional integration and international liberalization on the space economy within a country are investigated.

Chapter 4 mainly develops an analytical model to explain industrial redispersion. Unskilled workers are assumed to be employed in both the traditional and manufacturing sectors. The analytical results could explain both why and where industrial agglomeration and dispersion arise.

Chapter 5 steps forward and analytically investigates the definition of home market effect. By employing one manufacturing sector and two production inputs, i.e. capital and labor, it can successfully be revealed that spatial disparity in terms of wage presents a bell-shape respect to regional integration. Moreover, using data from China, this book empirically studies the HME in terms of wages in the case of China using panel data for the period 1980–2012. During regional integration, regional inequality in wages between the coastal and interior regions seemed to evolve in an inverted U-shaped curve.

Chapter 6, the final chapter in this book, first summarizes the insights that have been illustrated in the various chapters and discusses implications relative to the NEG models. Finally, topics for further research are listed.

Chapter 2
Review of New Economic Geography

2.1 Introduction

Economic activities are always relevant to the two dimensions of time and space. While time is often integrated into economic theoretical considerations, the study of where economic activities take place is almost always ignored by mainstream economists. In fact, in the real world, spatial distributions of population and employment are never smooth. In addition to the uneven endowment of natural resources, economic forces called the second nature also play a dominant role in shaping economic geography. Though this subject was once regarded intractable, some exciting new models dealing with increasing returns and monopoly competition have emerged (Dixit and Stiglitz 1977). In the wave of increasing-returns revolution, the new trade and new growth theory are born successively. Based on them, Paul Krugman's seminal paper "Increasing returns and economic geography" (1991) endogenously reaped the mechanism of economic agglomeration and inaugurated the new era of spatial economics, which became known as New Economic Geography (NEG). Since then, a large amount of improved works under this framework have been developed to analyze the impacts of globalization and regional integration on the spatial economy.

It has been two decades since the birth of New Economical Geography. Its theoretical merits have encouraged mainstream economists to pay much more attention to the spatial dimension of the economy. NEG has been successful in offering rationales for the formation and existence of economic agglomeration or the cluster in geographical space. NEG provides an equilibrium framework to explain the market access forces pulling economic activities together and the market-crowding ones pushing them apart, resulting from the tradeoffs between increasing returns and mobility costs. Compared to its antecedents such as regional science and urban economics, NEG attempts to enter the black box of agglomeration economies and show the self-reinforcing character of spatial concentration from more fundamental considerations (Fujita et al. 1999, p. 4). Another merit of

J. Wang, *Economic Analysis of Industrial Agglomeration*,
https://doi.org/10.1007/978-981-10-7437-0_2

NEG is that the formation of economic agglomeration is derived explicitly based on a full micro foundation. Economic space is represented as the outcome of the equilibrium individual's interaction.

NEG's achievements attract more and more attention from mainstream economics. However, despite its countless refinements and rapid progress following Krugman's seminal paper, NEG still has some internal and external drawbacks and challenges. During the glorious process of advance, queries have always accompanied the progress. One question for NEG is that many of its stories about industrial agglomeration or cluster cannot explain the real countries and regions. The mismatch between its original theory and the real space-economy, as Krugman (2011) puts it, means that the NEG model has entered middle age and seems decreasingly applicable to actual location patterns of advanced nations. More than that, economic geographers complain that NEG overemphasizes the role of pure economic mechanism and neglects the complexities of geographical features. Even though the model is simple and illuminating, such models are unable to explain the rich and complex hierarchy that characterizes the space-economy (Ottaviano and Thisse 2004). NEG models really tell the story about why economic agglomeration occurs, but they have little concern about where the agglomerations arise. Most NEG models assume that there are only two regions and the distributions of economic activities are decided by pure economic power. In the real world, however, regional comparative advantages still play a non-trivial role through their interaction with the second nature (Fujita and Mori 2005). In NEG, homogeneity of location space is facilitated to investigate the complicated mechanism of economic agglomeration. However, it is too unrealistic to explain the real uneven world. The landscape of economy forms under a synthesis of the first nature and the second nature.

Nowadays, globalization has brought about manufacturing outsourcing and spreading from developed countries to developing ones. The emerging economies, especially the BRICS (Brazil, Russia, India, China and South Africa) countries, shoulder the main task of manufacturing production for the world. These economic powerhouses play an important role in the world's economic stage. When investigating the space-economy within these countries, economic geography seems reminiscent of the circumstance of developed nations at the beginning of the twentieth century (Krugman 2011). Economic landscape in these nations is reshaped in the process of international trade liberalization. For example, China's industrial growth and agglomeration has been accompanied by massive migrant labor from its hinterland to coastal regions where manufacturing industries are massively concentrated. Empirical evidence reveals that the regional disparity is increasing due to the economic liberalization and globalization between 1985 and 1994 in China (Fujita and Hu 2001). This means that the concept and approach of NEG is not outdated after all. China's industrial cluster and localization in its eastern region are the evidence to support NEG.

In addition, regional developments under economic integration exhibit differentiated responses across regions within a country. With the development of economy, especially the economic integration and the improvement of infrastructure within these countries, the relocation of manufacturing to hinterland is increasing in developing countries such as Mexico and Brazil (Hanson 1996; Henderson et al. 2001). In China, the growth rate of per capita GDP exhibited some convergence after the large gap from the late 1990s to 2006 between hinterland and coastal regions (Fan and Sun 2008). In addition to local government policy, industrial dispersion from east to west is a growing tendency in China. Fally et al. (2010) find that market and supplier access have a stronger positive impact on wage disparity across Brazil, and that there is higher population density in Brazil's coastal regions. Similarly, in a study of post-Soviet Leningrad Oblast, Golubchikov finds that in the integration under globalization, the geographical elements of region proximity and size is responsible for the formation of economic core and periphery (Golubchikov 2006). In these cases, the original core-periphery theory appears to be weak to explain the phenomenon of industry redispersion.

It is important to note that what happened in recent years in the real world proposes some new issues for NEG. The distribution of economic activity within a country is affected by the integration of international trade liberalization and the boost of domestic infrastructure simultaneously. Moreover, the domestic regions in these countries are asymmetrical in terms of their access to the overseas market. There are well-documented facts that the market accessibility of domestic regions has a significant impact on its trade volume and firm agglomeration. More importantly, the hinterlands in emerging economies are always endowed with more unskilled workers. Although NEG sets forth a pure economic theory to explain the formation of agglomeration, the weakest point of it is its geography. It is time to consider this limit in the explanation of spatial economy. As noted, earlier NEG literature focused on self-reinforcing mechanisms in reshaping spatial agglomeration. It is time for us to incorporate the omitted asymmetrical geographical features into the original theory to explain the increasing regional disparity in emerging countries in the process of globalization. It seems necessary to step out the assumption of only two regions, two industries and the iceberg transport cost.

Based on the above considerations, the purpose of this chapter is to present a detailed review of the refinements in NEG. As there are several profound surveys on the developments of NEG, this book focuses especially on geographic space. Early NEG models consider only two regions or countries that are symmetrical in terms of size and market access. After 20 years of developments, there appears an evolution from symmetry to asymmetry in NEG. The models having asymmetric assumptions begin to emerge. These models are becoming increasingly sophisticated. It is essential to sort out their typical papers and make some summarization. Although some works have attracted sufficient attention, we need to shed light on their future possibility. The remainder of the chapter is organized as follows. This book first describes the basic framework of NEG models in Sect. 2.2. To show the related developments of NEG, this chapter reviews the existing works and compares their differences in Sect. 2.3. In Sect. 2.4, this book provides a further research direction to consider full asymmetry. It emphasizes that the first nature advantage of regions plays a noteworthy role through its interaction with pure economic forces. If domestic regions are endowed with different regional scale and access to the world markets, a theory based on these assumptions will be much closer to reality. Finally, concluding remarks are given in Sect. 2.5.

2.2 The Framework of New Economic Geography

Krugman's seminal Core-Periphery (CP) model (1991) provides a basic framework for most NEG models. It clarifies how interactions among increasing returns and transport cost can result in the emergence and evolution of economic agglomeration. In this section, this book briefly reviews the basic NEG models. Although there are abundant extensions to the CP model, the structure of them is identical (Robert-Nicoud 2005). This book also introduces those extensions that step outside the canonical framework. Employing a quasi-linear utility function and linear transport costs, Ottaviano et al. (2002) bring fresh air to NEG, presenting analytical results regarded as a great breakthrough in NEG.

2.2.1 *The Core-Periphery Model*

The classic CP model (Krugman 1991) is considered the basis of NEG models. In it, the spatial economy consists of two regions that are evenly endowed with the same economic structure. There are two sectors in each region: one is the numéraire (e.g., agriculture) and another is manufacturing, respectively denoted A and M. The numéraire sector produces a unit of homogenous goods with constant-return-to-scale technology exploiting one unit of unskilled labor under perfect competition. A representative firm of the manufacturing sector supplies differentiated goods using skilled workers under monopolistic competition. All goods and skilled workers are mobile between the two regions, but unskilled workers are immobile.

(1) Consumption

A representative consumer in each region has the same CES (constant elasticity of substitution) utility function in the following form:

$$U = C_M^{\mu} C_A^{1-\mu}, \quad C_M = \left[\int_0^n q(i)^{1-\frac{1}{\sigma}} di \right]^{\frac{\sigma}{\sigma-1}}$$

where $q(i)$ and C_A denote the consumption of manufacturing goods variety i and numéraire goods, respectively, and $\mu (0 < \mu < 1)$ is a constant denoting the expenditure share of manufactured goods. n is the range of varieties produced, and parameter $\sigma (\sigma > 1)$ is the constant elasticity of substitution between any two varieties. $1 - 1/\sigma$ represents the intensity of the preference for variety in manufactured goods.

The consumer has a budget constraint given by $p_A C_A + \int_0^n p(i)q(i)di = Y$ where p_A and $p(i)$ are prices of numéraire goods and manufacturing goods variety i respectively; Y is his income. The consumer's problem is to maximize the utility function subject to the budget constraint by choosing his amount of consumption.

Following Fujita et al. (1999), we express the consumer's demands for numéraire and manufacturing goods as follows:

$$C_A = \frac{Y}{p_A}(1-\mu) \tag{2.1}$$

$$q(i) = \mu Y \frac{p(j)^{-\sigma}}{P^{-(\sigma-1)}} \tag{2.2}$$

where P is the price index for manufactured goods having the following form:

$$P = \left[\int_0^n p(i)^{1-\sigma} di\right]^{1/(1-\sigma)} \tag{2.3}$$

As is assumed in the standard models of New Economic Geography, each variety of manufacturing goods is produced in only one region where firms produce them with same technology and price. The manufacturing goods are traded between the two regions, which is associated with transport costs. The numéraire goods are freely transported between the regions, and their prices are equalized.

The iceberg form of transport costs is assumed for manufacturing goods, meaning that when goods are shipped from region r to region s, it is assumed that only a fraction $1/\tau_{rs}$ arrives. Here, τ_{rs} represents such a unit transport cost. It means that the price of goods consumed in region $s(p_{rs})$, which are produced in region r at price p_r, can be written as $p_{rs} = p_r \cdot \tau_{rs}$. This book denotes the number of varieties produced in region $r(s)$ by $n_r(n_s)$. Using Eq. (2.2), the demand function of consumers in region s for manufacturing goods produced in r can be expressed:

$$q_{rs}(j) = \frac{p_{rs}^{-\sigma}}{P_s^{1-\sigma}} \mu Y_s \tag{2.4}$$

Then the price index in region s can be written as:

$$P_s = \left[n_r(p_r \cdot \tau_{rs})^{1-\sigma} + n_s p_s^{1-\sigma}\right]^{\frac{1}{1-\sigma}} \tag{2.5}$$

The total demand in location r can be expressed as follows:

$$q_r = \mu \frac{p_{rs}^{-\sigma}}{P_s^{1-\sigma}} Y_s \cdot \tau_{rs} + \mu \frac{p_{rr}^{-\sigma}}{P_r^{1-\sigma}} Y_r \tag{2.6}$$

(2) Production

We now turn to the production side of the economy. The numéraire goods are produced with constant-returns-to-scale technology under perfect competition. This book assumes that one of unskilled workers produce only one unit of numéraire goods, and workers' wages in the two regions are equalized at one. To produce $q(i)$ amounts of manufacturing goods at region r, l^M amounts of labor are used, i.e.

$$l_r^M = \alpha + \beta q_r(i) \tag{2.7}$$

where α and β represent the fixed and marginal costs of manufacturing, respectively. The firm in region r determines its outputs so as to maximize its profit, written as follows:

$$\pi_r = p_r(i)q_r(i) - w_r(\alpha + \beta q_r(i)) \tag{2.8}$$

where w_r is the wage rate. Given the previous assumptions, profit maximization of the firm results in the price of its output as follows, and the price in region s can be written as

$$p_r = \frac{\sigma}{1-\sigma}\beta w_r \tag{2.9}$$

$$p_{rs} = \frac{\sigma}{1-\sigma}\beta w_r \cdot \tau_{rs} \tag{2.10}$$

Due to the free entry into market, the zero-profit condition exists, which yields the equilibrium output of the firm as follows:

$$q_r^* = \frac{\alpha(\sigma-1)}{\beta} \tag{2.11}$$

And the input of labor can be written as

$$l_r^M = \alpha + \beta q_r = \alpha\sigma \tag{2.12}$$

Denoting L_r^M to be the total number of manufacturing workers and the number of firms in region r by n_r,[1] it can be written as:

$$n_r = \frac{L_r^M}{l_r^M} = \frac{L_r^M}{\alpha\sigma} \tag{2.13}$$

Concerning the meanings of (2.4) and (2.13), some additional interpretations are worth putting forward. The number of varieties produced in a region is proportionate to the regional whole labor force. If we assume that all manufacturing goods

[1]One variety only is produced in one location, so the number of firms equals the number of variety.

are available at the same price, then from Eq. (2.4), P can be simply expressed as $P_r = p_r^M n^{1/1-\sigma}$. It means that the increase of manufacturing varieties will reduce the price index.

(3) Short-run equilibrium

For the manufacturing goods, using (2.6), the supply-demand balance condition gives:

$$q_r^* = \mu \frac{p_{rs}^{M-\sigma}}{P_s^{1-\sigma}} Y_s \cdot \tau_{rs} + \mu \frac{p_{rr}^{-\sigma}}{P_r^{1-\sigma}} Y_r \tag{2.14}$$

By using the equilibrium price p_r given by (2.9) and the NEG's traditional normalization of $\beta = (\sigma - 1)/\sigma$ and $\alpha = \mu/\sigma$ (see Fujita et al. 1999, p. 54) the instantaneous equilibrium wage and price index in region r can be written in a much simpler form. That is, the manufacturing wage for region r is given by

$$w_r = \left[\frac{Y_s \tau_{rs}^{1-\sigma}}{P_s^{1-\sigma}} + \frac{Y_r^{1-\sigma}}{P_r^{1-\sigma}} \right]^{1/\sigma} \tag{2.15}$$

and the price index becomes

$$P_r = \left[\frac{1}{\mu} L_s^M (w_s \tau_{sr})^{1-\sigma} + \frac{1}{\mu} L_r w_r^{1-\sigma} \right]^{\frac{1}{1-\sigma}} \tag{2.16}$$

where Y_s(or Y_r) is the income of consumers at region s (or r). According to the previous assumptions, the wage of numéraire is equal to 1. This book also assumes that the share of manufacturing workers is μ, and that of numéraire workers is $1 - \mu$ in the whole economy and that each region is evenly endowed with numéraire workers. Then, if the share of manufacturing workers in region r is denoted by λ_r, the income of region r can be written as

$$Y_r = \mu \lambda_r w_r^M + 1 - \mu \tag{2.17}$$

Following the established tradition in NEG, in the short run it is assumed that markets can adjust instantaneously. Here the spatial allocation of manufacturing workers is considered as given. The wage of manufacturing workers, the price index and the workers' income of each are determined in the instantaneous equilibrium at a point in time.

(4) Long-run equilibrium

In the previously described short-run equilibrium, the migration of skilled workers between regions is not considered, and the manufacturing distribution is fixed at one point in time. As time passes, the distribution of manufacturing workers will change across the two regions. Workers will move between them according to the indirect utility differential.

As the result of utility maximization, we can express the indirect utility of an industrial worker in region r using income, manufacturing price index and price of numéraire goods as follows:

$$V_r = w_r P^{-\mu} p_A^{-(1-\mu)} \tag{2.18}$$

In the long run, skilled workers migrate between regions seeking higher indirect utility. As $p_A = 1$ and the indirect utility (V_r) means the real wage ω_r, which is the nominal wage deflated by the cost of living index P^{μ}, we have

$$V_r = \omega_r = \frac{w_r}{P^{\mu}} \tag{2.19}$$

Just like Baldwin et al. (2003, p. 15), we can express the migration equation of skilled workers as

$$\dot{\lambda}_r = (\omega_r - \omega_s)\lambda_r(1 - \lambda_r) \tag{2.20}$$

where λ_r represents the share of skilled workers in region r.

The real wages are determined by a system of Eqs. (2.15)–(2.17) and (2.19). Skilled workers can migrate between the two regions according to the difference of the real wages between them. Unfortunately, the simultaneous equations of (2.15)–(2.17) and (2.19) are too complicated for one to get the analytical solution, so numerical simulation is usually employed. The existing NEG models show how the decreases in transport cost affect the equilibrium distribution of manufacturing workers between the two regions, which can be demonstrated using the following two figures.

First of all, Fig. 2.1 plots the relocation between real wage differentials of two regions and the share of manufacturing workers in region r in accordance with different transport costs across regions. In the case of low transport costs, the curve of real wage differentials shows a unstable equilibrium point at S and the two stable ones at A and B, respectively. This means that all manufacturing workers would agglomerate to region r or to another region s. In the case of high transport costs, the curve of real wages differentials has only one stable equilibrium point S. This implies that both region r and s would have half of the whole manufacturing workers, i.e., industrial agglomeration would not occur. In the case of intermediate transport costs, there turns out to be three stable equilibrium points at G, S and H, and two unstable one at U_1 and U_2, respectively. This indicates that all manufacturing workers would agglomerate to region r and region s, or the two regions would have half of manufacturing workers at the same time.

Secondly, Fig. 2.2 shows the relation between the equilibrium share (λ_r) of manufacturing workers in region r and transport costs (τ_{rs}) across the region. From it, we can see that when transport costs are very high, the value of λ_r would be 1/2, which implies that region r and s would share half of manufacturing workers simultaneously. When transport costs are very low, the value of λ_r becomes 0 or 1.

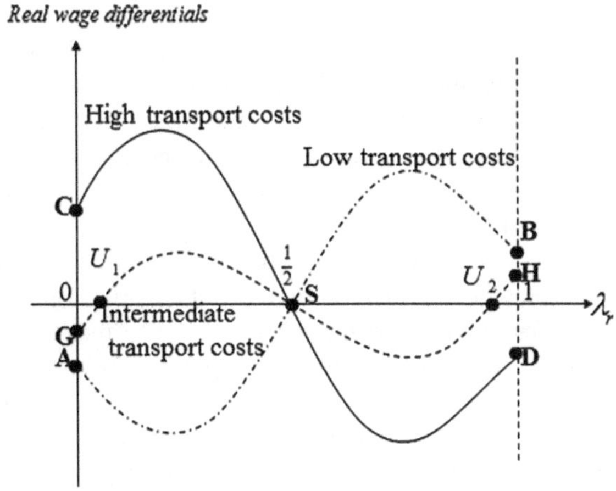

Fig. 2.1 The wiggle diagram and local stability (Baldwin et al. 2003, p. 26)

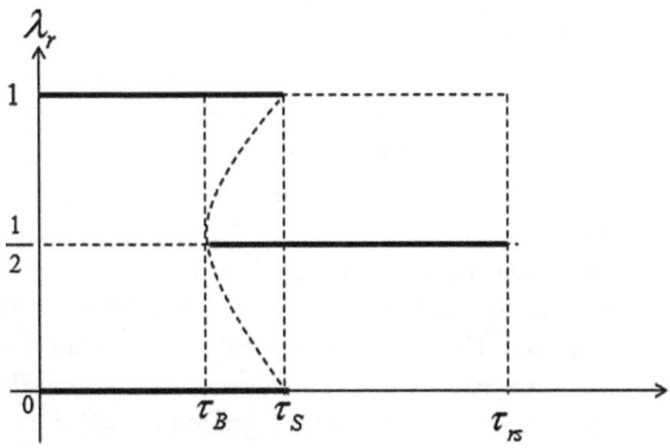

Fig. 2.2 The tomahawk diagram for core-periphery model

This means that all manufacturing workers would agglomerate to region r or to region s. It can also be seen that when transport costs are intermediate, say between τ_B and τ_S, the value of λ_r could be 0, 1/2 or 1. That is, there would be a full agglomeration of manufacturing workers in region r or region s, or there would be no agglomeration of them in either of the two regions. Here, τ_B and τ_S are called break point and sustain point, respectively, in NEG models.

Although the CP model is mathematically intractable, it conveys rich results and economic implications. Before the invention of analytical models, it enjoys popularity for many years. In the following, we review the refinements of the CP model.

2.2.2 The Refinements of the CP Model

Since the emergence of the CP model, the research issues of NEG have attracted concerns from mainstream economists. However, the problem of its mathematics and intractability hampers its further progress. To date, the original CP model has relied heavily on the tricks that are called, in Fujita et al. (1999), "Dixit-Stiglitz, icebergs, evolution, and the computer." To avoid the handicap of CES setup with iceberg-form transport cost, people incorporate an alternative of utility and technological hypothesis and investigate the robustness of the results. Based on the thread of the original CP model, countless refinements and extensions have been developed.

One of the most celebrated advances is the OTT model (Ottaviano et al. 2002). It steps out the original canonical framework, which incorporates distinctive consumer preference and transport costs. The merit of this model is mathematically tractable, which successfully incorporates the pro-competitive effect, i.e., decreasing profit-maximization in competition, which is a centrifugal force. Another distinction is that each consumer's spending on manufacturing varieties becomes independent of income, and the overlap originated from income effect disappears. But the OTT model still captures the main features of the original CP model.

Besides the OTT model, there are many other extensions on the basis of the CP model. They do not break away from the framework of "Cobb-Douglas-Dixit-Stiglitz-Iceberg" originally utilized in Krugman (1991). One is the footloose capital model, i.e. the FC model (Martin and Rogers 1995). The FC model abandons many remarkable features of the CP model in order to obtain its tractability. For example, the mobile factor repatriates all of its earnings to its original region, and the causality of demand and the cost links are disappearing. But, the CP model's agglomeration mechanism is kept in the FC model, which is related to the home market effect that a region's economic activities encourage more industries to locate in the region. The merits of the FC model entail that it can be used to deal with many asymmetrical cases. However, it is also worth noting that, as an important feature of the FC model is the migration capital, it is more suitable for the study of capital movement between two countries.

The merits of the CP model are plain to see, but its intractability prevents it from further spreading and providing more economic policy guidance. So, seeking its analytical model becomes the main task of spatial economists. Forslid and Ottaviano (2003) modify a CP model and develop the solvable version of the CP model called the FE model. It assumes that both skilled and unskilled workers are employed in the manufacturing sector. Krugman and Venables (1995) and Fujita et al. (1999) extend the original CP model to express the migration of factors by the input-output linkage among firms. The parallel of forgoing FE and FC models are FCVL (i.e. Footloose Capital Vertical Linkage) (Robert-Nicoud 2002) and FEVL (i.e. Footloose Entrepreneur Vertical Linkage) (Ottaviano 2002). Those vertical linkage models show the same insights as the CP model, while FCVL and FEVL yield tractable solutions.

There is another parallel of these models. Most NEG models indicate that spatial agglomeration is the result of globalization and economic integration. But, when we detect the spatial evolution of some developing countries, as mentioned before, redispersion from the core region to the periphery can be observed. Especially in recent years, the patterns of spatial economics are much richer than those of the CP model. Many firms are relocated from the core to the periphery. In other words, industrial dispersion takes place in congested core regions or cities. By now, some papers have investigated this process under the NEG framework. Tabuchi (1998) and Tabuchi and Thisse (2002) synthesize the NEG framework with urban economics and show that urban congestion costs can bring about redispersion of manufacturing with the decrease of transport costs. Picard and Zeng (2005) find that the agricultural sector can contribute to the redispersion of economic activities. Because of the requirement of agriculture labor in the manufacturing sector, two dispersion forces generated by the agriculture sector dominate the agglomeration forces. With further economic integration, relocation of manufacturing from the core to the hinterland is demonstrated. The changes of dispersion-agglomeration-redispersion seem to be a universal phenomenon. We need to employ new tools to explicitly explain the redispersion of spatial economy.

To date, the progress of NEG has been very fast. By using an alternative of utility functions and technological assumptions, NEG models have been improving. Nevertheless, this does not mean NEG has matured completely. When we review the existing models, we find that the FC model is more appropriate to investigate international trade, as it assumes that only goods but not workers are mobile between countries. Similarly, no production factors are mobile between countries in the FE model. But the international movement of capital such as FDI is an important feature of globalization. In this sense, NEG models have some application limits. Despite these drawbacks, we could still say the refinements of NEG models made so far have broadened and improved the explanation of spatial economics.

Since the emergence of CP model, many refinements have been made to explain the mechanism of economic agglomeration. Although these models show distinguished forms, their basic logic ideology still originates from Krugman's seminal paper. The models keep its typical features in their works and show many identical conclusions, but when we apply the alternative models of NEG, we find that the setting of two regions is unrealistic to explain the complex real spatial economy. In addition, as Ottaviano and Thisse (2004) point out, NEG allows one to better understand why agglomeration occurs; its models have little to say about where agglomeration arises. So it is needed to investigate why some regions are more successful than others. The setting with two regions is insufficient to explain the multi-regional system of the real economy. In most NEG models, the spatial economy is determined purely by economic mechanism.

The assumption of homogeneous space makes it easy to understand the mechanism of spatial agglomeration. However, there are some cases in which the geography (first nature) plays a more important role in shaping the landscape of spatial economy than the economic force (second nature). In fact, regions are never wholly symmetric with the same endowment, especially in terms of their trade accessibility to overseas markets and their scales.

2.3 From Symmetry to Asymmetry

As the foregoing discussion indicated, there are many situations in the real world in which the asymmetrical geographical features play a significant role in economic development. In particular, in the spatial economy of the emerging economies, core regions are more successful than others. Their natural advantages are the indispensable element for them to become economic centers. It has been shown that China's industrial production presents strong agglomeration in its east coastal region, and the regional disparity between the interior and coastal region has been increasing (Fujita and Hu 2001). Amiti and Javorcik (2008) show that access to customers and suppliers are the main determinants of FDI location in China.

There are many documents accounting for the impact of geographic handicaps on regional economic disparity. Gallup et al. (1999) find that geographic elements have major effects on economic growth through transportation costs and agriculture productivity. As Behrens and Gaigne (2006) discuss, some geographic elements, such as topography, climate and natural resources, are beyond the reach of economic policy. When we incorporate geographic features into our NEG models, the accessibility to main markets and regional sizes are important for economic consideration. Earlier assumptions of two symmetrical regions in early NEG models need to be modified. In this section, this book provides a detailed summary about the related literatures. These works are divided into symmetrical and asymmetrical cases based on how they deal with the accessibility to markets and region sizes.

2.3.1 *The Symmetrical Models*

So far, there have been a growing number of theoretical literatures about the spatial distribution of economic activities among countries or regions in NEG. However, owing to their different springboards and hypotheses, there has not yet been a unified explanation of the distribution of economic activities. Many earlier papers focused only on the case of two regions or two countries as with trade theory and investigated the domestic or international disparities. Meanwhile, a few works expand to include two countries or four regions. But, the regions and countries considered are still symmetrical in terms of access to markets and the size of regions and countries.

With respect to the earlier literature, symmetrical size and access of regions or countries are considered. Krugman (1991) initiates the classical CP model and endogenously reaps the economic agglomeration by utilizing monopolistic competition, increasing return to scale and iceberg-form transport costs. As a seminal paper, it inaugurates a new era, but the case of two symmetrical regions is investigated (see Fig. 2.3).

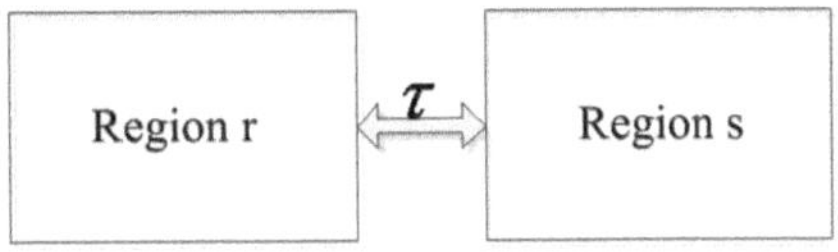

Fig. 2.3 The CP model. *Note* τ is the transport cost

Some other works focus on the industry agglomeration and relocation between countries (Martin and Rogers 1995; Puga 1999, Puga and Venables 1996). They explore only the economic agglomeration or dispersion at the level of regions or countries independently and fail to analyze them across regions and countries at the same time.

We note that some studies step forward and incorporate a setting of two domestic regions and consider the rest of world as the third region (see Fig. 2.4). Krugman and Livas (1996) use such a setting to show that closed markets encourage regional convergence while open markets disaggregate it by considering the urban land rent and commuting cost as a centrifugal force. In contrast, assuming that immobile workers are a centrifugal force, Paluzie (2001) reaches the opposite conclusion that trade liberalization exacerbates the regional inequalities within a country. In these models, although the impact of international trade on industrial location is considered, the two domestic regions are assumed to be endowed with identical size and access to the world market.

In a paper investigating spatial economy, Behrens (2011) incorporates two countries involving three regions, and finds a complex relationship between regional disparity and international trade costs and domestic transport cost. In his paper, two countries are considered, but regions are still symmetrical in terms of their sizes and accessibility to the world market.

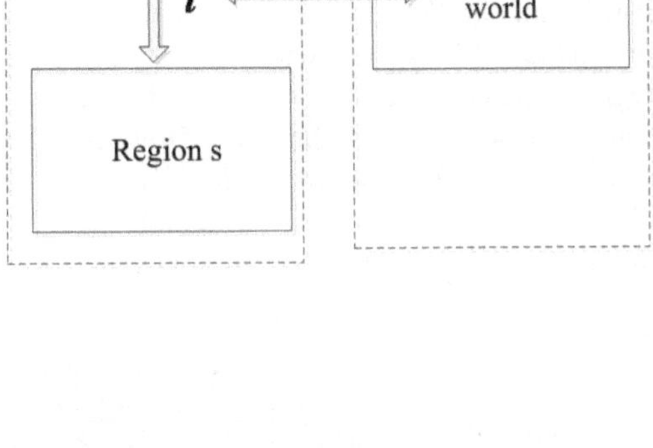

Fig. 2.4 A model of two countries and three regions. *Notes* t is the transport cost, T is the trade cost

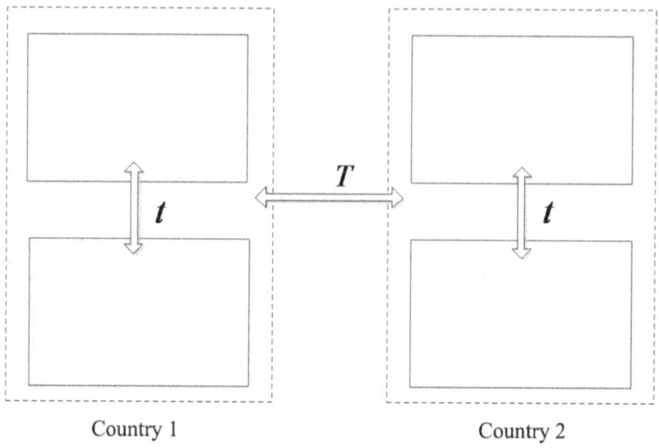

Fig. 2.5 A model of two countries and four regions. *Notes* t is the transport cost, T is the trade cost

A few other researchers present a framework having two countries and four regions (see Fig. 2.5). Monfort and Nicolini (2000) analyze such a framework and conclude that the economic integration of countries results in the emergence of regional economic agglomeration. Behrens et al. (2006b, 2007) successfully obtain an analytical result for such a model of two countries involving four regions using the quadratic utility function and linear transport costs. But in their papers, the domestic transport costs of the two countries are assumed to be equal. It is unrealistic that the two countries, such as a developed country and a developing one, have the same infrastructure level.

2.3.2 *The Asymmetrical Models*

Unlike the above-mentioned symmetrical models, some recent papers also pay much attention to geographical asymmetry by assuming a border region or hub. Ago et al. (2006) analyze the evolution of spatial economy in a model of three regions located on a line with a decline of transport cost. They show that the central region always has a location advantage, but it will weaken or even disappear by using a quadratic-linear function. However, there is no international trade considered in their model, and the regional sizes are equally assumed. Crozet and Koenig (2004) assume a border region in their model involving two domestic regions and the rest of the world, and demonstrate that domestic regional agglomeration

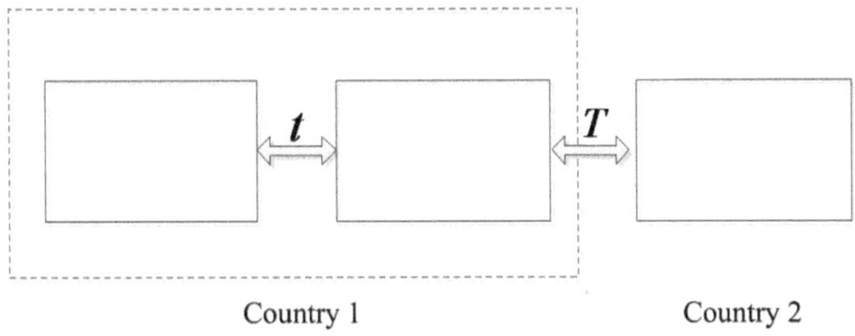

Fig. 2.6 The asymmetrical model of three regions. *Notes* t is the transport cost, T is the trade cost

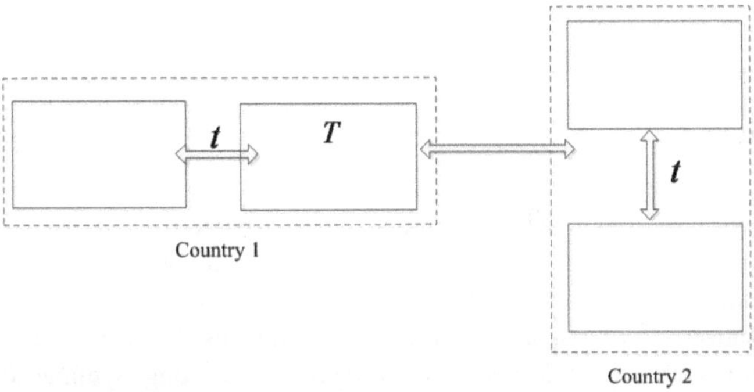

Fig. 2.7 The asymmetrical model of two countries and four regions (1). *Notes* t is the transport cost, T is the trade cost

depends only on the trade liberalization (Fig. 2.6). But in their paper, the effects of domestic transport costs are neglected. Behrens et al. (2006a) investigate the impacts of changes in domestic transport costs and international trade on regional industrial location (Fig. 2.7). The regions in a country have asymmetrical accessibility to overseas markets, but their size remains symmetrical.

Finally, Zeng and Zhao (2010) analyze the relation between the interregional (international) inequalities and international trade cost and domestic transport costs by assuming asymmetrical sizes of countries and regions (Fig. 2.8). Unfortunately, in their paper, regional accessibilities to overseas markets are still symmetrical.

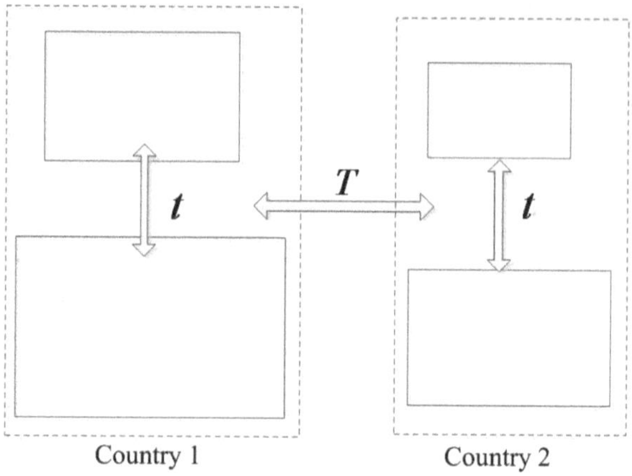

Fig. 2.8 The asymmetrical model of two countries and four regions (2). *Notes* t is the transport cost, T is the trade cost

2.4 Toward Full Asymmetry

As explained, NEG has reached a mature phase, especially from the viewpoint of the developments of its two-region models. However, these models are still unable to explain the complex and asymmetrical spatial economy. NEG offers a satisfactory explanation for why spatial agglomeration happens. But it has explained little about where such an agglomeration emerges. Its existing symmetrical models indicate that spatial agglomeration always emerges in one of the two regions. As Behrens et al. (2006b) point out, most NEG models expunge the geography by confirming themselves to "double-point economics." In fact, a tiny change of accessibility of domestic regions produces more abundant results than the basic CP model. Besides the asymmetry of accessibility, when size of regions and countries are assumed to be asymmetric, the region disparity can exhibit an inverted U-shape with respect to trade costs in the FC framework (Zeng and Zhao 2010). Existing research has not studied cases in which both regional sizes and accessibilities to overseas market are asymmetrical.

In the real world, the hierarchy of space economy is characterized by different accessibilities and sizes. In China, for example, coastal regions have better access to international markets, while more unskilled agriculture workers live in the hinterlands. This applies to other emerging economies in the world, as well. It is important to incorporate such a full asymmetry into the traditional NEG models to explain complex spatial economy.

As an attempt to accurately reveal the reality of developing countries like China, we could consider the home country has two asymmetrical regions. The hinterland region has to access to overseas markets through the gate region, and the former is also endowed with more unskilled workers than the latter (Fig. 2.9). We believe

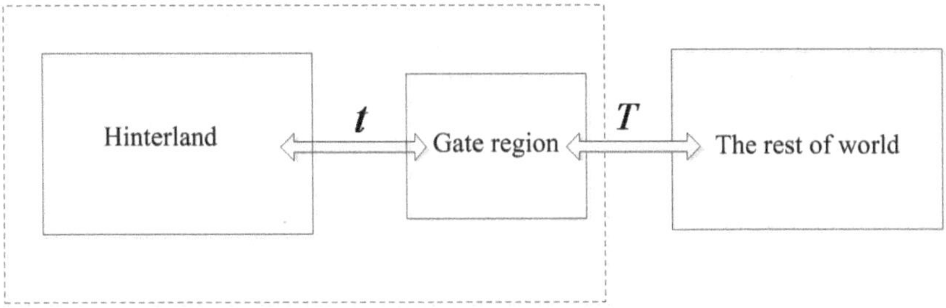

Fig. 2.9 A model of full asymmetrical regions. *Notes* t is the transport cost, T is the trade cost

that such an incorporation of regional asymmetry could contribute to the exiting theoretical models of NEG.

Forslid and Ottaviano (2003) present a model having asymmetrical regional sizes and find more abundant results than the symmetric CP model. As a result, the region with more immobile workers attracts a large number of manufacturing firms. This is because the centrifugal forces in NEG models are mainly the demands of immobile workers. In the reduction of transport costs, the region having many of those workers shows the advantage of attracting more manufacturing firms. Such an asymmetrical situation seems to be more prevalent in the developing world, especially in BRICs countries.

Furthermore, Behrens et al. (2006a) show that when the domestic regions are well integrated, firms prefer to locate in a region that has better access to overseas markets. It would be interesting to see what would happen if the hinterland were endowed with more immobile workers while the gated region had better accessibility. When we allow the hinterland to have different sizes, more interesting results may arise. Besides these asymmetrical considerations, to better explain the reality of developing countries, the agriculture sector is also worth being incorporated into NEG. It can be seen that unskilled workers are employed not only in the agriculture sector but also in the manufacturing one. These considerations could enrich the centrifugal forces in the interaction of economic activities. We hope to offer a better explanation about why spatial agglomeration happens and where it arises.

In the past three decades, China has experienced a rapid urbanization and an increasing regional disparity in globalization. But in recent years, dispersion of manufacturing industries is often mentioned by the media. In addition, the economic growth rates in the central and western provinces have become higher than eastern coast regions. Such a process of industrial dispersion attracts more attention from local governments and scholars. Regarding such a transition from agglomeration to dispersion, we need to give more explicit and persuasive explanation. At present, few works have been done to investigate such a dispersion process. It is obvious that the objective of firm migration is the seeking of a better location where the prices of labor are cheaper. This process also confirms the importance of comparative advantages, which means that to consider the full asymmetry would also help us to explore the recent industrial dispersion in China.

2.5 Concluding Remarks

NEG has been developing for two decades since the birth of Krugman's Core-Periphery model. It has conceptually matured and attracted much attention from mainstream economics. NEG employs the pure economic theories and successfully explains the endogenous formation of spatial agglomeration. But one of its weak points is geography. It remains unable to explain the real and complex hierarchy that characterizes the spatial economy. When we observe the space of the emerging economies, some core regions are more successful than others. The natural advantages of these regions are indispensable to their being economic centers. It is important to consider these natural advantages such as regional accessibilities and sizes in the explanation of spatial economy.

This chapter presented an overview on the recent developments of NEG and proposed some ideas about further research. Based on a retrospect of the developments of NEG, this book found that many existing models are isomorphic, showing identical results in a similar way. The existing two-region model is very useful, but there is still a gap between theory and reality. For this reason, this book thinks that it is needed to consider the full asymmetry in terms of regional accessibilities and sizes in NEG. This book hopes to use this approach to better explain the recent dispersion of manufacturing activities in many emerging countries in the near future.

Chapter 3
Industrial Agglomeration: A Simulation Model

3.1 Introduction

It has been two decades since the birth of New Economic Geography (hereafter, NEG). Over the past two decades, the work undertaken by NEG has inspired a much-needed examination of spatial aspects of the economy. There is no doubt that NEG has its theoretical and practical merits, offering a way for pure economic models to explain spatial agglomeration of economic activities. However, the progress of this work has been questioned. For instance, a kind of question about NEG has arisen that many stories about industry agglomeration or clusters have faded away in more advanced economies (Krugman 2011). Furthermore, the treatment of geographic space and location as simple two points is often singled out for criticism by economic geographers (Garretsen and Martin 2010). Have NEG's method already become out-of-date and inapplicable?

Globalization has in fact led to increased outsourcing in manufacturing, which has spread from the developed to the developing world. Emerging economies, especially the BRICS countries, bear the brunt of manufacturing for the world. When investigating the space-economy within these emerging economies, especially in China,it is found that the spatial economy is highly reminiscent of the space-economy of advanced countries around 1900 (Krugman 2011). The spatial evolution of the manufacturing sector in these emerging nations offers another template for verifying the framework of NEG. For example, China's economic growth and industrial agglomeration are accompanied by massive migrant labor from the hinterland to coastal regions where manufacturing industries are concentrated. Empirical evidence reveals that the increasing regional disparity is attributed to economic liberalization and globalization between 1985 and 1994 in China (Fujita and Hu 2001). Similar developments are also found in Brazil and other emerging countries. Fally et al. (2010) indicate that market and supplier access have a stronger positive impact on the wage disparity across Brazil, and there is higher population density in coastal regions.

J. Wang, *Economic Analysis of Industrial Agglomeration*,
https://doi.org/10.1007/978-981-10-7437-0_3

Upon closer inspection, geography itself indeed plays an important role in the reshaping of the industrial economic landscape. In a study of the post-Soviet Leningrad Oblast Golubchikov (2006) finds that in the integration into the world economy, geographical elements such as regional proximity and size account for the formation of economic core periphery. The differences of trade costs seem to be vital to regions within a country. Economic landscapes in these nations were reshaped in the process of international trade liberalization and domestic regional integration. In retrospect, prior NEG literature placed more emphasis on consideration of self-reinforcing mechanisms in economic spatial agglomeration. It is time for us to incorporate the omitted asymmetrical geographical features into the original theory, in order to explain increasing regional disparity in countries in the process of international trade liberalization and domestic regional integration. In addition, it is worth noting that the traditional models of NEG were built on the basis of simple two region comparison. As Fujita and Mori (2005) stated, it is imperative to go beyond the simple two-region models and use an asymmetric many-region models of trade and geography in order to acquire practical and useful policy implications. Although there are many attempts to investigate the case of multi-regions (Paluzie 2001; Monfort and Nicolini 2000), unfortunately there is little consideration of full asymmetry, and of the fact that the market size and trade accessibility are both different, NEG models tell the story of why economic agglomeration occurs, but they are largely unconcerned with where the agglomerations arise.

To answer this latter question, this chapter attempts to adapt the NEG model to interpret spatial evolution in developing countries such as China. This chapter considers that both the size and accessibility of regions within a country are asymmetrical. For instance, the gate region has better access to overseas markets and the hinterland has a greater share of unskilled workers. By means of simulation, two key results are obtained. First, when international trade liberalization continues but domestic regions remain poorly integrated, the gate region experiences a change from partial to full agglomeration. Second, when a country is closed to global markets, regional integration makes the hinterland attract a great share of manufacturing firms. However, when a country is extremely open to global markets, full agglomeration of manufacturing firms occurs in the gate region.

The remainder of this chapter is organized as follows. In Sect. 3.2, a detailed review of related literature is provided. Section 3.3 extends the original NEG model to a two-country and three-region case where domestic regions are fully asymmetrical in terms of their sizes and the accessibility to global markets. In Sect. 3.4, the relationship between the spatial distributions of manufacturing, regional integration, and international globalization is investigated using simulation methods. Section 3.5 concludes this chapter.

3.2 Related Literature

Recently, a growing number of theoretical works have emerged addressing the spatial distribution of economic activities in NEG. However, due to differentiated models and methods, these works have not provided an explicit picture of the distribution of economic activities. In the earlier literature, symmetrical sizes and accessibilities of regions or countries are always considered. Krugman (1991) initiates a classical core-periphery model and endogenously explains the economic agglomeration by utilizing monopolistic competition, increasing returns to scale, and iceberg transport cost. In his work, however, only two symmetrical regions are considered. There are many other works on industrial agglomeration (Martin and Rogers 1995; Puga 1999; Puga and Venables 1996). These works mainly explored industrial agglomeration or dispersion across regions or countries, but they did not analyze these developments across regions and countries simultaneously.

Some studies have emerged and incorporated a setting with two domestic regions and the rest of world as the third region. Krugman and Livas (1996) show that a closed market encourages regional convergence, while an open market causes regional divergence. Paluzie (2001) reaches an opposite conclusion: that trade liberalization exacerbates the regional inequalities within a country. A few other studies expand these models to a framework with two countries and four regions. Monfort and Nicolini (2000) point out that the process of integration between countries results in the emergence of regional economic agglomeration. Behrens et al. (2006b, 2007) successfully obtains the analytical results for this kind of models using a quadratic utility function and linear transport costs. Furthermore, Behrens (2011) consider a model of two countries involving three regions, as does this book, to show the complex relationship between regional disparity and international trade costs and domestic transport cost. In Behrens's model, however, the regions of each country are symmetrical in terms of their sizes and accessibilities.

Unlike these symmetrical models, some recent papers have paid attention to the geographical asymmetry, assuming a border region or hub. Ago et al. (2006) analyze the evolution of space economy of three regions located on a line. This study shows that the central region always has a location advantage, but it may be weakened and even disappear. Unfortunately, no international trade is considered in their model, and regions are equally endowed with sizes. Crozet and Koenig (2004) consider a border region in their model of two domestic regions and the rest of the world. They show that domestic regional agglomeration depends on the trade liberalization, neglecting the effects of domestic transport costs. Behrens et al. (2006a) investigate the impact of changes in domestic transport costs and international trade on industrial location. The regions considered have asymmetrical access to global markets, but their sizes remain symmetrical. Zeng and Zhao (2010) analyze the relation between the interregional (international) inequalities and international trade costs and domestic transport costs among countries and regions with asymmetrical sizes. However, in this study regional accessibilities to overseas markets are still symmetrical.

In summary, the existing works have not studied a case in which regional sizes and accessibilities to global market are asymmetrical. In this chapter, Krugman's classic framework (1991) is applied to investigate the complex relationship between trade and transport costs and the spatial economy within a country by assuming that domestic regions are asymmetrical in terms of their sizes and accessibilities. This assumption of full asymmetry is closer to the reality of developing countries, like China. In most developing economies, a country can always be divided into the gate region and the hinterland one, where economic actors in hinterland have to pass through the gate region to access to the world market, and the hinterland also contains more unskilled workers than the gate region. We believe that incorporating these asymmetrical assumptions will contribute to the existing theoretical studies of NEG.

3.3 The Model

The classic core-periphery model (Krugman 1991), which is considered as the gauge of NEG model, is adopted in our spatial economy of two countries involving three regions. Specifically, our model embraces consideration of geographical features to theoretical analysis. The spatial economy consists of two regions within a country i.e., the hinterland (H) and the gate region (G) and the rest of the world (R). The gate region (G) exhibits a geographical advantage in terms of better access to the world market, whereas economic actors in the hinterland (H) have to go through the gate region to the global market. The two domestic regions have different regional sizes as well as different levels of accessibility (Fig. 3.1).

There are two sectors in each region: numéraire (e.g., agriculture) and manufacturing, denoted by A and M respectively. The numéraire sector produces a unit of homogenous goods with constant-return-to-scale technology by using one unit of unskilled labor under perfect competition. A representative firm of the manufacturing sector supplies a differentiated good using skilled worker under monopolistic

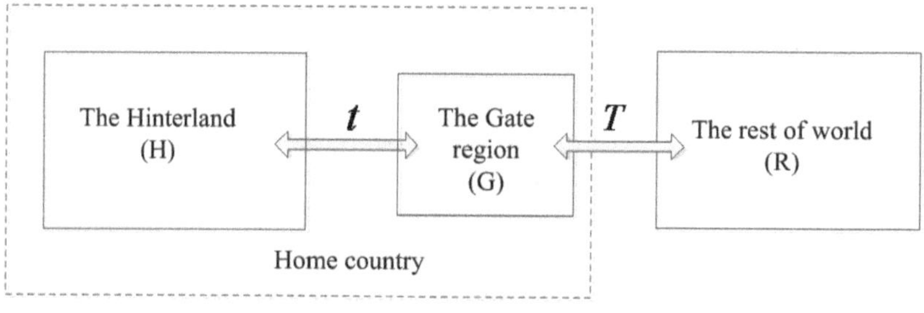

Fig. 3.1 A model of two countries and three regions. *Notes* t is the interregional transport cost, and T is the international trade cost

competition. All goods are mobile among the three regions. The skilled workers can only migrate across domestic regions, whereas unskilled workers are immobile.

The population of the world is normalized to 1, and if the share of skilled workers is denoted by μ, the ratio between unskilled and skilled workers is $(1-\mu)/\mu$. In a home country, the hinterland is unevenly endowed with a higher share of unskilled workers than the gate region. The number of skilled workers located at region s $\left(L_s^M\right)$ can be written as $L_s^M = \lambda_s\mu$, $(s = H, G, R)$, where λ_s means the share of skilled workers in region s, which will be endogenously determined in the model.

3.3.1 Consumer Behavior

A representative individual in each region has the same CES utility function as the following form:

$$U = \frac{1}{\mu^\mu(1-\mu)^{1-\mu}}\left[\int_0^n q(i)^{1-\frac{1}{\sigma}}di\right]^{\frac{\sigma\mu}{\sigma-1}} C_A^{1-\mu}$$

where $q(i)$ and C_A denote the consumptions of the ith variety of manufacturing good and numéraire goods respectively, and $\mu(0<\mu<1)$ is a constant denoting the expenditure share of manufactured goods. n is the range of varieties produced, σ $(\sigma > 1)$ means the constant elasticity of substitution between any two manufacturing varieties and $1-1/\sigma$ represents the intensity of the preference for the variety of manufactured goods.

The consumer maximizes his utility function subject to a budget constraint given by $p_A C_A + \int_0^n p(i)q(i)di = Y$ where p_A and $p(i)$ are the prices of numéraire goods and manufacturing goods respectively, and Y is the consumer's income.

Following Fujita et al. (1999), we can obtain the consumer's demand function for numéraire and manufacturing goods respectively as follows:

$$C_A = \frac{Y(1-\mu)}{p_A} \tag{3.1}$$

$$q(i) = \mu Y\frac{p(i)^{-\sigma}}{P^{-(\sigma-1)}},\ \text{for}\ i \in [0, n] \tag{3.2}$$

where P is the price index of manufactured goods which has the following expression:

$$P = \left[\int_0^n p(i)^{1-\sigma}di\right]^{1/(1-\sigma)} \tag{3.3}$$

3.3.2 Trade and Transportation Costs

As in the standard model of NEG, each manufacturing variety is assumed to be produced at only one location. Manufacturing goods can be traded among the three regions and consequently incur trade or transport costs. The numéraire goods are freely transported among the regions and their price is equalized among the three regions as one, i.e., $p_s^A = 1, s = H, G, R$.

As in Krugman (1991), this book assumes the iceberg form of transport costs for manufacturing goods. If one unit is shipped from region r to region s, only a fraction of it $(1/\tau_{rs})$ arrives. Here, the constant τ_{rs} represents the transport cost. So, for a good produced at region r and transported to s, its price at region s can be written as $p_{rs} = p_r \cdot \tau_{rs}$. T and t denote the international trade and domestic transport costs respectively. The transport cost τ_{rs} can be classified into the following three cases:

$$\tau_{rs} = \begin{cases} T & \textit{if } r = G, s = R \textit{ or } r = R,\ s = G \\ t & \textit{if } r = H, s = G \textit{ or } r = G,\ s = H \\ T \cdot t & \textit{if } r = H, s = R \textit{ or } r = R,\ s = H \end{cases} \tag{3.4}$$

Using (3.2), the consumer's demand function at region s for manufacturing goods produced at region r becomes:

$$q_{rs}(i) = \frac{(p_r \tau_{rs})^{-\sigma}}{P_s^{1-\sigma}} \mu Y_s \tag{3.5}$$

Using (3.3), then the price index at region s can be written as:

$$P_s = \left[\int_0^{n_G} (p_G(i) \cdot \tau_{Gs})^{1-\sigma} di + \int_0^{n_H} (p_H(i) \cdot \tau_{Hs})^{1-\sigma} di + \int_0^{n_R} (p_R(i) \cdot \tau_{Rs})^{1-\sigma} di\right]^{\frac{1}{1-\sigma}}, \quad s = G, H, R \tag{3.6}$$

Based on (3.5), the total amount of demand at region r can be expressed as following:

$$q_r^M = \mu\left(\frac{(p_r \tau_{rG})^{-\sigma}}{P_G^{1-\sigma}} Y_G \tau_{rG} + \frac{(p_r \tau_{rH})^{-\sigma}}{P_H^{1-\sigma}} Y_H \tau_{rH} + \frac{(p_r \tau_{rR})^{-\sigma}}{P_R^{1-\sigma}} Y_R \tau_{rR}\right), r = G, H, R \tag{3.7}$$

3.3.3 Producer Behavior

We now turn to the production side of the economy. We assume that numéraire goods are produced with constant-returns-to-scale technology under perfect competition. One unskilled worker is used to produce one unit of numéraire goods, and his wages in the three regions are equalized to 1. To produce $q_r^M(i)$ amounts of manufacturing goods at region r, the following inputs of skilled workers is needed:

$$l_r^M = \alpha + \beta q_r^M(i) \tag{3.8}$$

where α and β implies the fixed and marginal costs of manufacturing. The firm chooses its optimal inputs so as to maximize its profit denoted as follows:

$$\pi_r = p_r^M(i) q_r^M(i) - w_r^M \left(\alpha + \beta q_r^M(i)\right) \tag{3.9}$$

where $p_r^M(i)$ is the price of manufacturing good variety i, and w_r^M is the wage rate paid to skilled workers. Under the monopolistic competition, the profit maximization of the firm gives the price of manufacturing goods as follows:

$$p_r^M = \frac{\sigma}{1-\sigma} \beta w_r^M \tag{3.10}$$

So, the price of such goods produced at region r but to be sold at region s has the following expression:

$$p_{rs}^M = \frac{\sigma}{1-\sigma} \beta w_r^M \cdot \tau_{rs} \tag{3.11}$$

Suppose that there is free entry and exit of firms into and out of market and that zero-profit condition exists, which yields the equilibrium output of the firm as follows:

$$q_r^{M*} = \frac{\alpha(\sigma - 1)}{\beta} \tag{3.12}$$

Using L_r^M to denote the number of manufacturing workers and n_r to be the number of firms at region r, the labor market equilibrium gives the number of manufacturing firms or varieties at region r as follows:

$$n_r = \frac{L_r^M}{l_r^M} = \frac{L_r^M}{\alpha\sigma} \tag{3.13}$$

This means that the number of varieties produced at a region is proportion to the number of regional labor force. We assume that if all manufacturing goods are produced at the same price (p_r^M), then from (3.3) the price index of manufacturing goods can be simply expressed as $P_r = p_r^M n_r^{1/1-\sigma}$. Therefore, the increase of manufacturing varieties will reduce the price index.

3.3.4 Short-Run Equilibrium

For the manufacturing goods, using (3.7) and (3.12), the equality of supply and demand gives:

$$q_r^{M*} = q_r^M, \; r = G, H, R \tag{3.14}$$

By using the equilibrium price p_r^M in (3.10), the equilibrium output in (3.12), and the normalization result that $\beta = (\sigma - 1)/\sigma$ and $\alpha = \mu/\sigma$ (Fujita et al.1999, P.54), the instantaneous equilibrium wage at region r can be written as follows:

$$w_r^M = \left[\frac{Y_G(\tau_{rG})^{1-\sigma}}{P_G^{1-\sigma}} + \frac{Y_H(\tau_{rH})^{1-\sigma}}{P_H^{1-\sigma}} + \frac{Y_R(\tau_{rR})^{1-\sigma}}{P_R^{1-\sigma}} \right]^{1/\sigma}, r = G, H, R \tag{3.15}$$

and the price index at region r becomes:

$$P_r = \left[\frac{1}{\mu} \cdot L_G^M \cdot \left(w_G^M \cdot \tau_{Gr}\right)^{1-\sigma} + L_H^M \cdot \left(w_H^M \cdot \tau_{Hr}\right)^{1-\sigma} + L_R^M \cdot \left(w_R^M \cdot \tau_{Rr}\right)^{1-\sigma} \right]^{\frac{1}{1-\sigma}}, \quad r = G, H, R \tag{3.16}$$

Since the number of skilled workers located at each region s is $L_s^M = \lambda_s \mu$, the price index at region r turns into:

$$P_r = \left[\lambda_G \left(w_G^M \tau_{Gr}\right)^{1-\sigma} + \lambda_H \left(w_H^M \tau_{Hr}\right)^{1-\sigma} + \lambda_R \left(w_R^M \tau_{Rr}\right)^{1-\sigma} \right]^{\frac{1}{1-\sigma}}, r = G, H, R \tag{3.17}$$

Note that the wage of unskilled workers equals 1. We have also assumed that the share of skilled workers is μ and that of unskilled workers is $1 - \mu$ in the whole economy. Then, the income at region r can be written as:

$$Y_r = \mu \lambda_r w_r^M + L_r^A, \; r = G, H, R \tag{3.18}$$

where L_r^A is the share of unskilled workers at region r.

Following an established tradition in NEG, it is assumed that in the short run allocation of goods can be adjusted instantaneously. However, the spatial allocation of skilled workers is taken as given, or their migration across regions is ignored. That is, the income, the wage of skilled workers, and the price index of manufacturing goods of each region are determined as an instantaneous equilibrium at a point in time.

3.4 Industrial Spatial Configuration

The previous section described the short-run equilibrium. However, the migration of skilled workers between domestic regions and the resulting manufacturing distribution is not considered herein. In the long run, the distribution of manufacturing workers between the two domestic regions can be determined according to real wage differential between them.

3.4.1 Long-Run Equilibrium

In the long run, skilled workers migrate between regions seeking for higher real wages. As the result of utility maximization, we can express the indirect utility using income, manufacturing price index, and the price of numéraire goods for a consumer at region r as follows:

$$V_r = Y_r P_r^{-\mu} p_A^{-(1-\mu)} \tag{3.19}$$

Since $Y_r = w_r^M$, $p_A = 1$ the indirect utility just equals the real wage (ω_r), which is the nominal wage deflated by price index P^μ, i.e.:

$$V_r = \omega_r^M = \frac{w_r^M}{P_r^\mu} \tag{3.20}$$

The real wages can be determined by a system involving Eqs. (3.15), (3.17), (3.18), and (3.20). Skilled workers migrate between domestic regions so as to gain higher real wages. Unfortunately, the system of simultaneous equations is too complicated to reach the analytical solution. Like Krugman (1991), this book has to make use of numerical simulation to show some interesting results, which allow us to find how international trade liberalization and regional integration affect the equilibrium distribution of manufacturing between domestic regions.

3.4.2 Simulation Results

In our numerical simulation, this book assumes that $\mu = 0.4$ and $\sigma = 6$, following Paluzie (2001). Since there are no migrations of skilled workers between the home country and the rest of world, we fix the share of skilled workers of the rest of the world, i.e., λ_R to be $4/5$.[1] Therefore, the sum of the share of skilled workers of the home country becomes $1/5$. The share of skilled workers of the gate region is λ_G,

[1]Concerning the distribution of population between the home country and rest of the world, here this book assumes that the share of skilled and unskilled workers is in line with the reality of China's distribution. According to statistics provided by the World Bank (http://data.worldbank.org/), the rural and urban populations of China account for 22.4 and 17.52 percent respectively of the world's rural and urban population on averaged between 2001 and 2010. Accordingly, here this book assumes that the share of skilled and unskilled workers in the home country both occupy around one-fifth of the world's population in our simulation.

and that of the hinterland is $\lambda_H = 1/5 - \lambda_G$. The equilibrium distribution λ_G of manufacturing firms will be determined as the equilibrium results from the system of the simultaneous Eqs. (3.15), (3.17), (3.18), and (3.20), which indicate how the manufacturing industry is distributed between the gate and the hinterland regions.

As for the shares of unskilled workers in the three regions, we note that of the rest of the world can be written as $L_R^A = 4(1-\mu)/5$. To express the asymmetry of regional sizes, we assume that the share of unskilled workers of the hinterland region is $L_H^A = (1-\mu)/10 + \delta$, and that of the gate region is $L_G^A = (1-\mu)/10 - \delta$ with $\delta > 0$. That is, the scale of unskilled workers of the hinterland region is larger than that of the gate region. Here, $L_H^A + L_G^A = (1-\mu)/5$ means the whole sum of unskilled workers in home country is fixed. δ is assumed to be 0.012.[2] The varying parameters in our model simulations are international trade cost (T) and interregional transport cost (t). To see the impacts of trade liberalization and regional integration on manufacturing distribution within the home country, we vary values of T and t to represent different degrees of international openness and domestic infrastructure, and we obtain the simulation results shown in Table 3.1.

Table 3.1 shows the stable interior equilibrium values of the share of manufacturing industry (i.e., skilled workers) in the gate region. Horizontal and vertical directions indicate the different value of international trade cost and interregional transport cost, respectively. There are three types of equilibrium configurations obtained: stable equilibrium (SE), multiple equilibrium (ME), and core-periphery equilibrium (CP-E). Among three types of equilibrium, the SE and C-PE correspond to higher or lower transport costs. For intermediate values of transport costs, we have multiple equilibrium (ME). In the appendix, based on the simulation results, this book presents a number of figures to show how the real wage differentials between the gate and hinterland regions are related to the gate region's shares of skilled workers (or manufacturing industry) for the three types of equilibrium configurations. When domestic regions are endowed with different regional sizes and accessibilities, we have a richer array of results. For different values of trade costs and transport costs, we obtain various spatial variations and characters.

When international trade costs change, the spatial configurations show different patterns. For example, when the home country is poorly integrated (e.g., $t > 1.65$), SE becomes the main pattern, and the stable interior equilibrium values of λ_G are getting

[2]According to the Chinese provincial statistical yearbook, the share of agricultural workers (unskilled workers) in the inland provinces is higher than that in coastal provinces by about 22.3 percent on average from 2001 to 2010. If we consider the phenomenon of larger rural migrant workers from hinterland to urbanized coastal provinces in China, the share of unskilled workers is greater in the hinterland compared to the coastal regions by close to 20 percent. Therefore, the total share of unskilled workers in China is $(1-\mu)/5$. The share of unskilled workers in hinterland and gate regions can be noted as $(1-\mu)/10 + \delta$ and $(1-\mu)/10 - \delta$ respectively. 2δ represents the difference of unskilled workers between the hinterland and the gate regions. Because in our simulation μ is assumed to be 0.4, then the total share of unskilled workers in China $(1-\mu)/5$ takes the value of 0.12. This means that more shares of 20 percent of unskilled workers in the hinterland equals 0.024. We can then say that $2\delta = 0.024 (\delta = 0.012)$ can reflect the reality of asymmetry in terms of regional size between the hinterland and gate regions in China.

Table 3.1 Equilibrium configuration types of manufacturing distributions

		T							
		1.85	1.75	1.65	1.55	1.45	1.35	1.25	1.15
t	1.85	SE 0.046	SE 0.047	SE 0.053	SE 0.064	SE 0.079	SE 0.126	ME 0.152	CPE G
	1.75	SE 0.044	SE 0.045	SE 0.047	SE 0.058	SE 0.075	SE 0.132	CPE G	CPE G
	1.65	ME 0.042	ME 0.043	ME 0.045	ME 0.047	SE 0.071	ME 0.141	CPE G	CPE G
	1.55	CPE G/H	CPE G/H	CPE G/H	CPE G/H	CPE G/H	CPE G	CPE G	CPE G
	1.45	CPE G/H	CPE G/H	CPE G/H	CPE G/H	CPE G/H	CPE G	CPE G	CPE G
	1.35	CPE G/H	CPE G/H	CPE G/H	CPE G/H	CPE G/H	CPE G	CPE G	CPE G
	1.25	CPE G/H	CPE G/H	CPE G/H	CPE G/H	CPE G/H	CPE G	CPE G	CPE G
	1.15	CPE G/H	CPE G/H	CPE G/H	CPE G/H	CPE G/H	CPE G	CPE G	CPE G

Note SE means stable equilibrium, ME means multiple equilibrium, and C-PE means core periphery equilibrium. Here, the pattern of G in CPE means agglomeration occurs only in the gate region and G/H either in the gate region or hinterland region

larger when international trade costs (T) is lower. With a further decrease of international trade costs (e.g., $T = 1.15, t = 1.85$), the differential of real wage between the gate region and hinterland becomes completely positive (see Fig. 3.11 in Appendix). This means that all manufacturing would agglomerate to the gate region.

Based on the simulation results shown by Table 3.1, Fig. 3.2 shows how international trade liberalization affects the distribution of manufacturing within the home country under high transport costs.[3] In Fig. 3.2, the heavy curved line indicates stable equilibrium (SE), and the heavy lines core-periphery equilibrium (C-PE). When the home country is poorly integrated ($t > 1.65$), stable interior equilibrium values of λ_G becomes larger as international trade costs are reduced. This means that more and more manufacturing firms would likely relocate to the gate region. When international trade costs are extremely low, the core-periphery pattern occurs only in the gate region.

It is necessary to note that when domestic regions are well integrated ($t < 1.65$), a full agglomeration of manufacturing in either the gate region or the hinterland is the spatial pattern of equilibrium as international trade costs decrease. However, when

[3]In Fig. 3.2, we should note that for the different value of t the corresponding thresholds of break and sustain points (T_B and T_S) are also different. In other words, these thresholds are the function of t. For the whole interval of $t > 1.65$, Fig. 3.2 just illustrates the general relationship between the share of manufacturing firms in the gate region and the trade costs. This note can also apply to Fig. 3.3.

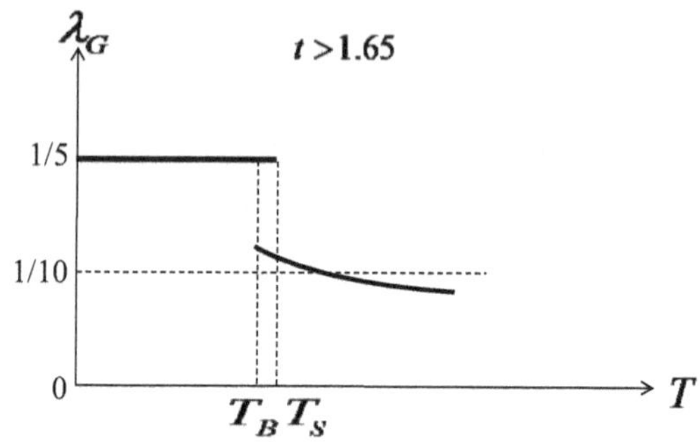

Fig. 3.2 The gate region's share of manufacturing firms (λ_G) when t is high

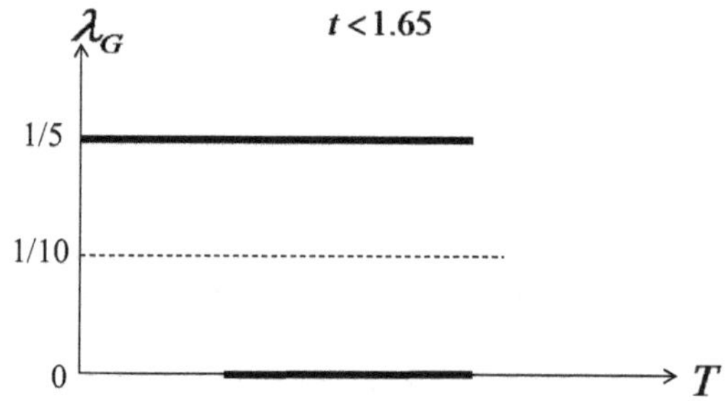

Fig. 3.3 The gate region's share of manufacturing firms (λ_G) when t is low

international trade costs are very low, the agglomeration only occurs in the gate region. This situation is shown in the Fig. 3.3.

When we investigate the spatial configuration by considering the decrease of interregional transport costs under different international trade costs, more interesting patterns arise. First, let us see the case that the economy of the home country is relatively closed to the overseas markets (say $T > 1.45$).Along with the decreasing of domestic transport costs, the spatial configurations change for different values of transport costs (also see Figs. 3.6, 3.7 and 3.8 in Appendix). When transport costs are very high, (e.g., $t = 1.85$), the stable interior equilibrium (SE) is the only pattern. With integration between domestic regions, the stable interior equilibrium value of λ_G decreases, implying that some manufacturing firms are relocating to the hinterland. When transport costs reach some intermediate values, we could have a multiple equilibrium pattern. With a further lower transport costs, e.g., $t < 1.55$, we have Core-periphery equilibrium in which manufacturing firms are located either in the gate region or the hinterland. These simulation results can be illustrated in Fig. 3.4, which is similar to the tomahawk diagram in the NEG literature.

It is important to note that Fig. 3.4 shows two sustain points (t_s^H and t_s^G) and a single break point (t_B),[4] but the stable interior equilibrium values of λ_G is

[4]Similar to Fig. 3.2, we should note that in Fig. 3.4 for the different value of T, the thresholds (t_B and t_S) could vary with the values of T. That is to say these thresholds are the functions of T. Figure 3.4 just illustrates the general relationship between the share of manufacturing firms in the gate region and the domestic transport costs. This note can also apply to Fig. 3.5.

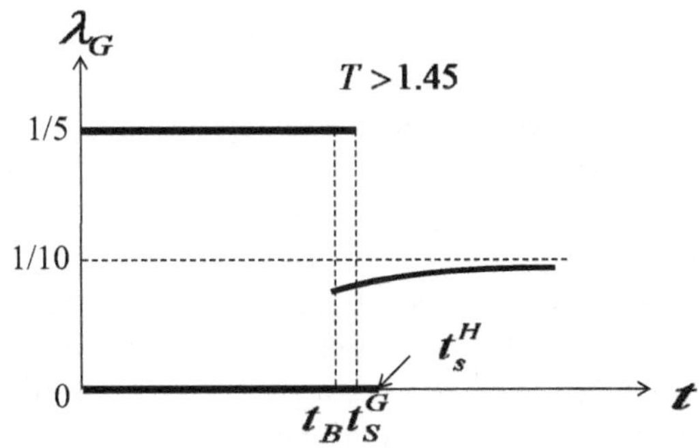

Fig. 3.4 The gate region's share of manufacturing firms (λ_G) when T is high

decreasing. This means that starting from higher interregional transport costs, a reduction of transport costs leads a small share of manufacturing firms to relocate from the gate region to the hinterland. The bifurcation in the figure shows that the spatial economy has multiple equilibrium (ME) and core-periphery equilibrium (C-PE) when surpassing the break point, t_B. Unlike the existing symmetrical CP models, we have two sustain points, and the large region, i.e., the hinterland, could become the core. That is, the industrial agglomeration in the hinterland is more likely to take place. As domestic transport costs decrease, the hinterland attracts a greater share of manufacturing when the home country is closed to global markets.

When the home country is open enough to the overseas market (e.g., $T < 1.45$), we could have different spatial patterns. Let us start from higher transport cost, e.g., $t = 1.85$. The interior equilibrium of the manufacturing share in the gate region is stable. But a reduction of transport costs would push some manufacturing firms to move from the hinterland to the gate region. As the reduction of transport cost continues, the spatial economy becomes multiple equilibrium and core-periphery equilibrium (also see Figs. 3.9, 3.10 and 3.11 in Appendix). When transport costs are very low (e.g., $t < 1.55$), the CPE occurs and the differential of real wage between the gate region and hinterland is completely positive. Consequently, all manufacturing firms would agglomerate to the gate region. However, unlike the previous case in which the home country is closed to global markets, here a full agglomeration of industry in the gate region is the only pattern. These simulation results are illustrated in Fig. 3.5.

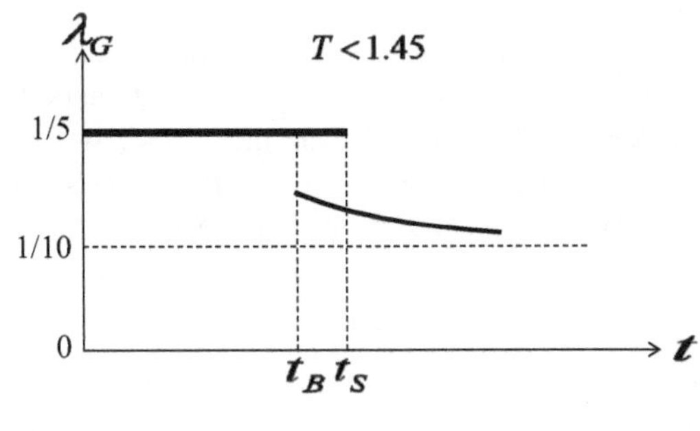

Fig. 3.5 The gate region's share of manufacturing firms (λ_G) when T is low

3.4.3 Interpretations and Discussions

In this section, this book first explains how international trade liberalization affects the location of industry within the home country (see Fig. 3.2). As illustrated in Forslid and Ottaviano (2003), because the hinterland has a greater share of unskilled workers, the market size of the hinterland is larger than that of the gate region. When the international trade costs and domestic transport costs remain high simultaneously, the market access advantage of the exogenously larger market size in the hinterland attracts a greater share of mobile firms. Therefore, if the initial stable interior equilibrium values of λ_G are smaller, the hinterland hosts greater than half of manufacturing firms.

When international trade liberalization continues but domestic regions remain poorly integrated, the gate region can provide better market access to manufacturing firms, because it is easy to export to overseas market. At the moment, the large overseas demand for manufacturing products will push manufacturing firms towards the low-cost, accessible gate region. The market access stemming from large market size in the hinterland is defeated by the better access to world market in the gate region. The asymmetry of access to the overseas market means manufacturing firms prefer the gate region in order to reduce international trade costs. With further integration of regions into the world market, the full concentration of firms in the gate region only arises when the international trade costs are significantly low.

In the prior related literature, such as Paluzie (2001) and Crozet and Koenig (2004), it is shown that the spatial distribution of firms within a country is affected only by international trade costs. In this book, we have shown that a tiny change in domestic transport costs may cause great changes to the spatial structure (see Figs. 3.4 and 3.5). Assuming asymmetrical regional sizes, the hinterland has a larger local market than the gate region. In the presence of transport costs, firms prefer to locate in the larger market because location in large market can save transport costs. When the home country is closed from the rest of world, the access advantage of the gate region becomes less important than the advantage of market size in hinterland. The hinterland could attract greater shares of firms to locate than the gate region. As transport costs fall but the trade costs remain high, a full agglomeration of firms would occur either in the gate region or the hinterland eventually, but the full agglomeration in the larger hinterland is much more likely (see Fig. 3.4).

In contrast, when the home country is open to world markets, the market access stemming from better access to world market in the gate region dominates the market size advantage of the hinterland. As in the Fig. 3.2, because in our model the population of the rest of world is considerably larger than that of the home country, the demands from the rest of world would promote firms to locate in the gate region where they can benefit from reduced international trade costs. Although the hinterland is endowed with a larger market size, the absolute advantage of market access in the gate region promotes a full agglomeration that occurs in the gate region only when the domestic transport costs are extremely low (see Fig. 3.5).

Based on the forgoing discussions, we see that the industrial agglomeration or dispersion within the home country is jointly determined by international trade costs and domestic transport costs. Unlike the prior NEG literature, we find that the gate region cannot necessarily always dominate the space of a country during the regional integration. Distinct international trade environments have different effects on industrial distribution. In particular, when domestic regions are poorly integrated, the decreasing of international trade costs would accelerate the industrial relocation to the gate region. These results are consistent with the recent industrialization process in China. Fujita and Hu (2001) indicate that China's regional disparity between coastal and hinterland regions has been increasing, with many manufacturing industries agglomerated in the coastal region. However, it is also found that when a country is extremely isolated from global markets, the hinterland attracts a greater share of industry than the gate region during the regional integration. As highlighted by Krugman and Livas (1996), Mexico City has a massive population but is far away from the US border before international liberalization. Similarly, Gallup et al. (1999) argue that in sub-Saharan Africa and some regions in Easter Europe the share of population living near to coastal or ocean-navigable river is not high. High levels of domestic transports and isolation from the overseas markets result in such agglomeration in the hinterland. Gallup et al.'s study further shows that agglomeration is likely to take place in a region with better accessibility when interregional transport costs and international trade costs are low enough. This is consistent with this chapter's conclusion based on Fig. 3.4.

3.5 Concluding Remarks

In this chapter, this book investigated the industrial agglomeration within a country under trade liberalization and interregional integration. Krugman's original NEG model was extended to a case of two countries involving three regions, in which the home country's two regions are asymmetrical in terms of their sizes and accessibility to the global market. The simulation results show that the spatial economy of the home country changes in a more complex way than is shown in Krugman's results. Compared to the original symmetrical core-periphery model, these results appear to be richer and closer to the real world.

The main results are as follows. First, when the home country is poorly integrated, its gate region experiences a change from a partial to a full agglomeration.

This means that when domestic transport costs remain very high, international trade liberalization accelerates firm relocation to the gate region. Second, when the home country is closed to global markets, the hinterland attracts more manufacturing as transports costs decrease. With a further reduction of transport costs, all manufacturing would agglomerate either in the gate region or the hinterland. However, when the home country is open to global markets, the full agglomeration occurs only in the gate region.

Appendix 1: Figures of Real Wage Differentials

1.1: The cases of higher international trade costs ($T > 1.45$) (Fig. 3.6, 3.7 and 3.8)

Fig. 3.6 Real wage differential of stable equilibrium (SE)

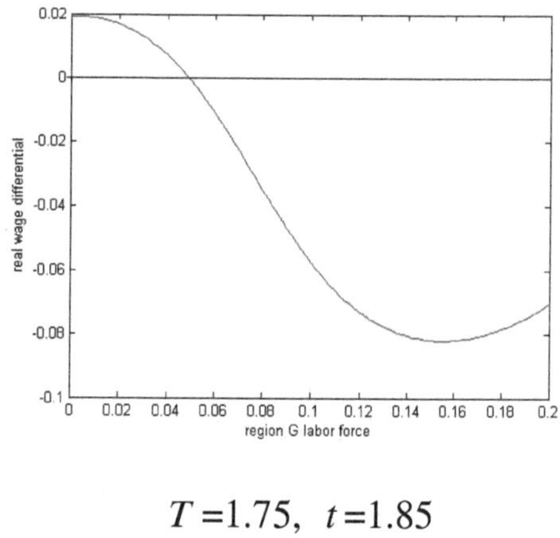

Fig. 3.7 Real wage differential of multiple equilibrium (ME)

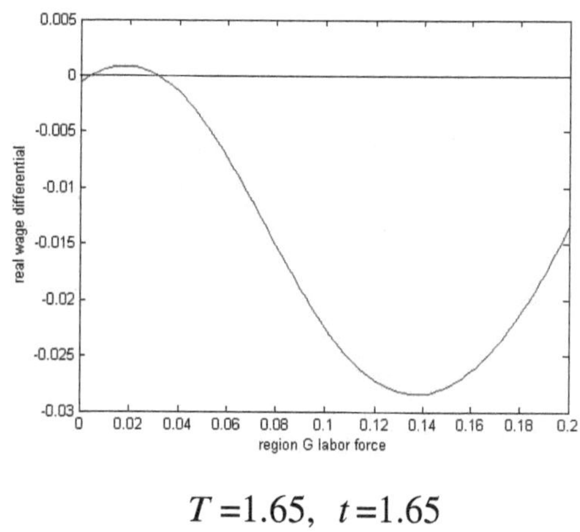

Fig. 3.8 Real wage differential of Core-periphery equilibrium (C-PE)

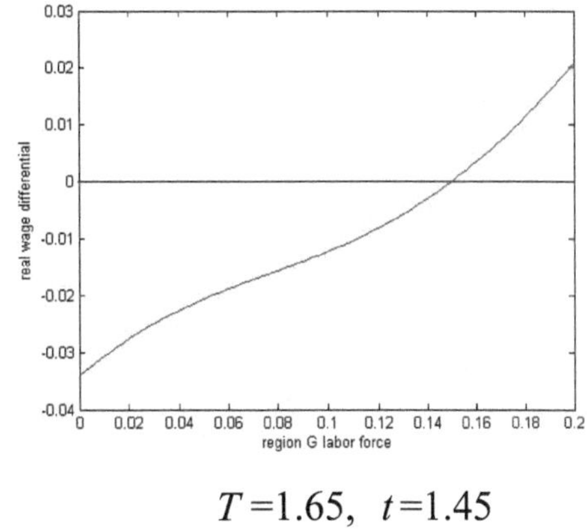

1.2: The cases of lower international trade costs ($T < 1.45$) (Fig. 3.9, 3.10 and 3.11)

Fig. 3.9 Real wage differential of stable equilibrium (SE)

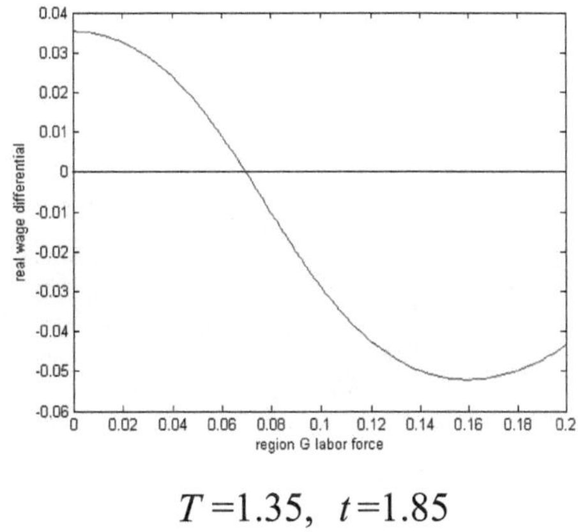

Fig. 3.10 Real wage differential of multiple equilibrium (ME)

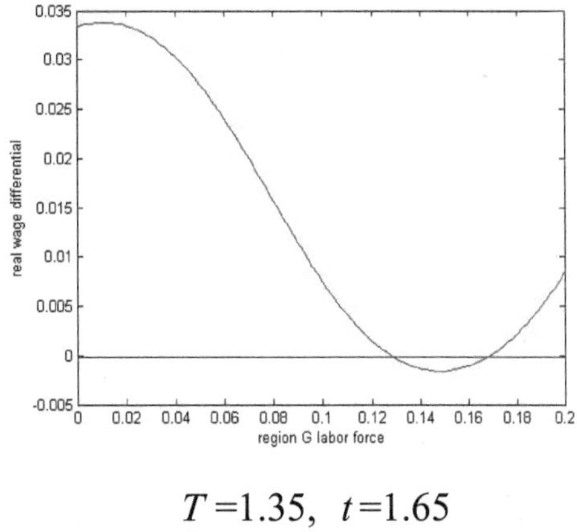

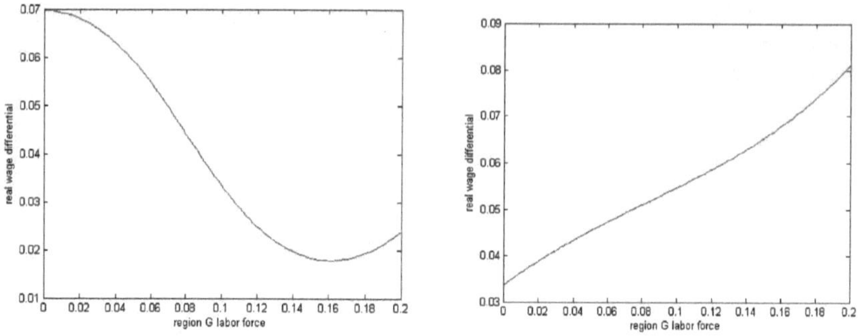

T=1.15, t=1.85 T=1.25, t=1.45

Fig. 3.11 Real wage differential of Core-periphery equilibrium (C-PE)

Chapter 4
Industrial Dispersion: An Analytical Model

4.1 Introduction

The main conclusions of early NEG models (Krugman 1991; Ottaviano et al. 2002; Forslid and Ottaviano 2003) tell us that high transport costs lead to the dispersion of industry in two symmetrical regions and that industrial agglomeration occurs when transport costs are low. This is also known as the core-periphery theory. As economic integration proceeds, we must ask: after the core-periphery what will the pattern of industrial distribution be, and how will the economic landscape change over time? Moreover, with agglomeration increasing, the greater concentrations of firms and mobile workers in the core regions will lead to the rise of extra costs related to production and living, such as workers' wages, higher land rents, and commuting costs. The further integration between regions causes the core regions to become over-concentrated, and some industries will tend to relocate to the periphery. That is to say that the evolution of spatial development undergoes a bell-shaped process in the long term. When we investigate the space economy of cities or regions within a country, we find that industrial deconcentration and the growth of hinterland regions do not seem to be exclusive phenomena. It has been observed that in some developed countries, such as the United Kingdom, the space economy has experienced the process of industrial redispersion (Geyer and Kontuly 1996). Similarly, there is ample evidence to show that manufacturing activities in the United States were heavily agglomerated in the Northeast and Great Lakes in the 1950s. In the ensuing decades, manufacturing has clearly become much more dispersed, and firms are much more spread out to the other parts of the country (Holmes and Stevens 2004). Also, industrial relocation from the central region to the hinterlands has even been witnessed in some emerging economies. As demonstrated by Haddad et al. (2002), the southern regions of Brazil actually experienced industrial redispersion due to the improvement of infrastructure and regional integration. Note also that Deichmann et al. (2005) investigated the issue of industrial relocation in Indonesia and found that the potential improvements in

J. Wang, *Economic Analysis of Industrial Agglomeration*,
https://doi.org/10.1007/978-981-10-7437-0_4

transport encouraged firm relocation from the core region to the lagging eastern part of the country. Given the facts outlined above, as Williamson (1965) observed, countries first go through a period of regional inequality and industrial agglomeration in some specific region and then experience industrial deconcentration and a move towards regional convergence as economic development proceeds. From the foregoing discussion, empirical evidence supports the idea that industry tends to agglomerate in some specific urban areas or regions during the initial stage of industrialization and that some industries then relocate to hinterland regions away from congestion or the higher-waged core region.

It goes without saying that the theory of New Economic Geography (Krugman 1991) has been successful in providing the rationales for the occurrence of economic agglomeration. NEG models tell us why agglomeration occurs, but they are largely unconcerned with where the agglomeration arises. In the early core-periphery models, the decrease in transport costs led to industrial agglomeration in one of the two regions. In other words, the two homogeneous regions seem to enjoy the same opportunity to become the center. This is obviously inconsistent with the real economic world. Generally speaking, the natural advantages of a region play important roles in choosing the center through their interaction with pure economic forces. Empirical evidence reveals that the regional disparity increased due to economic liberalization and globalization between 1985 and 1994 in China and that massive manufacturing firms agglomerated near the coastal regions, which have better access to the overseas markets (Fujita and Hu 2001). Similarly, Gallup et al. (1999) argue that in sub-Saharan Africa and some regions in Eastern Europe, the share of the population living near to coastal areas or ocean-navigable rivers is not high. The extremely high international trade costs and domestic transport costs result in such agglomeration within the hinterland. They further show that agglomeration is likely to take place in the region that has better accessibility when interregional transport costs and international trade costs are low enough. Thus, we find that the occurrence of industrial agglomeration is not equally likely in any location. The agglomeration generally arises in specific locations that are endowed with certain natural advantages, such as transport accessibility.

As Behrens et al. (2006a) discussed, NEG has allowed us to combine old ingredients via a new recipe to explain the formation of economic agglomeration, and the weak point of the NEG theory is geography itself. When we investigate developed core regions, we find that they are always endowed with some inherent advantage, such as natural resources or a good location for transport. However, most NEG models rely heavily on the abstract two-region model for deducing analytical tractability. As Fujita and Mori (2005) advocated, it is imperative to go beyond the simple two-region models and use asymmetric many-region models of trade and geography in order to acquire practical and useful policy implications. We need to give an explicit picture of industrial location during trade liberalization and regional integration. The same is true of the models of industrial redispersion. The related models of industrial redispersion are able to offer a reasonable mechanism explaining the occurrence of industrial deconcentration. Their weakest point is that they fail to tell us where the agglomeration occurs and where deconcentration comes from. Regarding the research into industrial redispersion, Tabuchi (1998) observes industrial redispersion by incorporating the urban costs as additional centrifugal forces. Furthermore, Tabuchi and Thisse (2002) show that the distribution of industry and trade costs presents a bell-shaped relationship when taste heterogeneity is employed in their model. It is worth mentioning that Picard and Zeng (2005,2010) investigate the process of industrial redispersion by considering the agricultural sector and a different production technique. Although these researches give reasonable explanations for redispersion, where the agglomeration arises and where redispersion originates are also at issue. In terms of spatial set-up, only a hypothetical two-region economy is investigated. In contrast to symmetrical considerations, Behrens et al. (2006a) incorporate geographic features into the NEG model. It is a pity that we could not witness the process of redispersion and that the full agglomeration is always in the gate region, even if the transport costs are extremely low.

To settle the foregoing issues, it is necessary to add geographical elements into the original NEG models to explain the explicit industrial location pattern, especially the process of industrial redispersion. The present chapter attempts to merge the study of industrial redispersion and geographical features within a single model. This book develops a three-region model based on Picard and Zeng (2010). Unskilled workers are invested both in the traditional sector and in manufacturing firms. This is consistent with the situation in most developing countries, where unskilled workers are massively employed in producing low-end manufacturing goods. More than that, this book considers a two-country, three-region case in which the home country is asymmetric in terms of its access to overseas markets. This allows us to analyze the impacts of inherent geography on the reshaping of space economy, along with the joint role of economic mechanisms. Because there are various spatial scales in our model, we are able to investigate the complicated interactions between international trade liberalization and regional integration, as well as their effect on the distribution of industry.

Using this framework, the analytical results reveal that there are abundant location patterns resulting from the process of globalization and regional integration. This book finds that when the home country is closed to global markets, poor domestic infrastructure allows the hinterland attract all of the manufacturing firms. With the further integration of the domestic economy, there will be a balanced distribution of industry between the gate region and the hinterland. When the country is open to global markets, starting with full agglomeration in the hinterland, a decrease in transport costs will trigger the firms to gradually move to the gate region during the integration of domestic regions. When this happens, the full concentration in the gate region will be maintained for a long while, even though the decrease in transport costs continues. With further regional economic integration, half of firms will relocate to the hinterland once again, with the other half of them remaining in the gate region.

The remainder of this chapter is structured as follows. A three-region theoretical model is presented in Sect. 4.2. In Sects. 4.3 and 4.4, this book analyzes the impacts of trade liberalization and regional integration on industrial location within a country. Section 4.5 provides a brief summary.

4.2 The Model

This chapter extends the work of Picard and Zeng (2010) to a richer spatial setting and consider a spatial economy consisting of two domestic regions denoted H and G, i.e., the hinterland, the gate region, and the rest of the world (henceforth, R). Regions G and H are located in the home country. In the following, variables associated with each region will be subscripted accordingly. The gate region (G) in the domestic economy exhibits a geographical advantage in terms of better access to world markets, whereas those in the hinterland must go through the gate region to reach the overseas markets. The geographical access to trade and transportation is illustrated in Fig. 4.1. There are two production factors in the economy: geographically mobile skilled workers and immobile unskilled workers. This chapter denotes the mass of skilled workers and unskilled workers in the three regions by L_G (resp.A_G), L_H (resp.A_H), and L_R (resp.A_R), respectively. This chapter assumes that the immobile unskilled workers, A, are evenly split between the domestic regions H and G, which means that $A_H = A_G$. In addition to these assumptions, the workers are supposed to be internationally immobile. Hence, the masses of skilled workers in the home country ($L = L_G + L_H$) and the rest of the world (L_R) are considered to be given and fixed. There are two production sectors in each region. The traditional sector only employs unskilled workers at constant returns to scale and supplies a traditional good under perfect competition. The second sector, called the manufacturing sector, produces a mass N of a variety of differentiated manufacturing good under increasing returns to scale and sells its products under monopolistic competition.

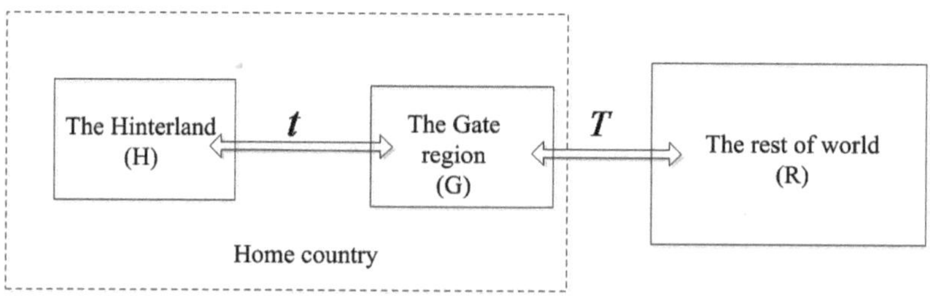

Fig. 4.1 A model of two countries and three regions. *Notes* t is the interregional transport cost, and T is the international trade cost

All products can be traded across countries and regions and consequently incur various unit transport costs. Traditional goods are freely transported between the regions. Transporting differentiated manufacturing goods across regions is costly. More precisely, this book assumes a unit of transport cost of $t > 0$ for shipping any variety of good between domestic regions, whereas transporting manufacturing goods from the gate region to rest of the world entails a unit trade cost of $T > 0$. Because this book assumes that transporting manufacturing goods from hinterland H to R requires going through gate region G, this implies that firms located in region H incur trade costs of $T+t$ to access the external global market. Here, transport costs reflect the level of infrastructure in the home country, and trade costs express the freeness of international trade, i.e., tariffs, transport costs, and even service costs. Given our assumption of asymmetric transport costs, we have:

$$\tau_{rs} = \begin{cases} T & \text{if } r = G, s = R \text{ or } r = R,\ s = G \\ t & \text{if } r = H, s = G \text{ or } r = G,\ s = H \\ T+t & \text{if } r = H, s = R \text{ or } r = R,\ s = H \end{cases}$$

4.2.1 Consumers

Each worker is endowed with one unit of labor and has quasi-linear preferences for three types of goods: manufacturing goods ($q(i)$), traditional goods (q_G^A, q_H^A and q_R^A), and homogenous goods (q_0) as a numéraire. As in Picard and Zeng (2010), a typical consumer in region r has the following quasi-linear utility with a quadratic sub-utility function and chooses her consumption problem:

$$U = \alpha \int_0^N q_r(v)dv - \frac{\beta-\gamma}{2}\int_0^N [q_r(v)]^2 dv - \frac{\gamma}{2}\left[\int_0^N q_r(v)dv\right]^2 + \left[q_G^A - \frac{1}{2}(q_G^A)^2\right]$$
$$+ \left[q_H^A - \frac{1}{2}(q_H^A)^2\right] + \left[q_R^A - \frac{1}{2}(q_R^A)^2\right] + q_0$$
$$s.t. \quad \int_0^N p_r(v)q_r(v)dv + p_G^A q_G^A + p_H^A q_H^A + p_R^A q_R^A + q_0 = y_r + \bar{q}_0$$

where $\alpha > 0$ measures the intensity of the preference for the differentiated products, and $\beta - \gamma > 0$ implies that skilled workers have a preference for variety. q_r^A denotes the consumption of traditional varieties of goods, which are perfectly differentiated and respectively produced at a constant returns-to-scale sector in the region $r = H, G, R$. $p_r(v)$ is the consumer price of variety v in region r, and y_r is the consumer's earnings, which depends on his or her skilled/unskilled status. In addition, q_0 is the consumption of the homogenous good that is used as a numéraire good. Each worker is endowed with $\bar{q}_0$ initial units of the numéraire, which is supposed to be large enough for consumption. Finally, the numéraire is assumed to be transported at zero cost. Its price can be normalized to one without losing generality.

Using these notations, each consumer maximizes his or her utility given budget constraints. It is readily verified that the linear demand function of manufacturing varieties in region r is as follows:

$$q_r(i) = a - (b + cN)p_r(i) + cP_r \tag{4.1}$$

where a,b, and c are positive coefficients given by

$$a = \frac{\alpha}{\beta - (N-1)\gamma}, \ b = \frac{1}{\beta + (N-1)\gamma}, \ c = \frac{\gamma}{(\beta - \gamma)[\beta + (N-1)\gamma]}$$

And where

$$P_r = \int_0^N p_r(v)dv \tag{4.2}$$

is the aggregate price index of the differentiated industry in region r. Then, $\bar{P}_r = P_r/N$ can be interpreted as the average price of the manufacturing products in region r.

Meanwhile, the first-order conditions of the consumer plan yield the individual demand for varieties of goods from the traditional sector in region r. Let p_r^A be the price of traditional varieties of goods produced in region r. Then, the individual demands in region r are simply given by

$$q_r^A = 1 - p_r^A \tag{4.3}$$

4.2.2 *Productions*

Turning to the supply side, this chapter assumes that product markets are segmented and that labor markets are made up of two groups of workers. Skilled workers are perfectly mobile between the domestic regions, and immobile unskilled workers exist only in local supplies. There are two kinds of sectors in the economy. The traditional sector requires one unit of A in order to produce one unit of output in any region. This represents free trade in traditional goods. In the other sector, the manufacturing sector, as in Forslid and Ottaviano (2003), both skilled and unskilled workers are employed as production investments. This chapter assumes that manufacturing technology requires one unit of L and ϕ units of local, immobile, unskilled workers as fixed costs. According to the NEG tradition, the marginal cost of production of variety is set to equal zero. Because the labor requirements of each firm are identical across the three regions, there is a one-to-one correspondence between the firm and variety. Thus, the number of manufacturing firms or varieties produced in region r equals the number of skilled workers. We denote the share of firms by $\lambda \in [0, 1]$ in the gate region of the home country.

$n_r(r = G, H, R)$ means the variety of goods produced in region r. Under these assumptions, labor market cleaning in each region implies that

$$n_G = \lambda L,\ n_H = (1 - \lambda)L,\ n_R = L_R \tag{4.4}$$

Then, we denote the market size of region r via $M_r = A_r + L_r$. Based on the foregoing notation, each firm's profit in region r, whose products are sold to the three regions, is equal to the revenues from sales minus the costs of both types of labor.

$$\pi_r = M_r p_{rr} q_{rr} + M_s(p_{rs} - \tau_{rs})q_{rs} - w_r^M - \phi w_r^A, s \neq r \tag{4.5}$$

where the first two terms refer to the firm's sales in local and other markets, and the last two terms refer to local factors' costs.

In the traditional sector, unskilled workers under the constant returns to scale produce one variety of traditional goods. Like Picard and Zeng (2010), this book assumes that each worker produces one unit of a traditional good. As the unskilled workers are supplied locally, traditional goods are distinguished according to the local endowment of the production factor.

4.2.3 Market Equilibrium

Each firm is assumed to choose its price by taking the price index as a given. Profit maximization implies optimal prices as follows:

Intraregional price:

$$p_{rr} = \frac{a + cP_r}{2(b + cN)} \tag{4.6}$$

Interregional price:

$$p_{rs} = p_{rr} + \frac{\tau_{rs}}{2} \tag{4.7}$$

Using the symmetry between firms, the aggregate price index (2) in region r can be written as

$$P_r = \int_0^{n_G} p_{Gr}(v)dv + \int_0^{n_H} p_{Hr}(v)dv + \int_0^{n_R} p_{Rr}(v)dv \tag{4.8}$$

After solving for the price equilibrium, the equilibrium wages in the manufacturing industry are determined by the zero profit condition, as is usual in a perfect labor market. Hence, there are no pure profits, so all operating profits are absorbed by the wage bill, which implies that

$$w_r^M = M_r p_{rr} q_{rr} + M_s (p_{rs} - \tau_{rs}) q_{rs} - \phi w_r^A \tag{4.9}$$

Because this chapter assumes that local factors are employed at unit productivity and zero transport costs for traditional goods, perfect competition in the markets of the traditional sector implies that the price of products is equal to the marginal costs. This means that

$$w_r^A = p_r^A \tag{4.10}$$

The individual demands for traditional goods in any region are as follows:

$$q_r^A = 1 - p_r^A = 1 - w_r^A \tag{4.11}$$

The total demand for traditional products in region r is equal to $q_r^A M$. Here, $M(M = M_G + M_H + M_R)$ means the total market size of all three regions. The supply of this good is equal to the number of units of local factor that are not used by manufacturing firms. As a consequence of market clearing, we can obtain:

$$q_r^A M = A_r - \lambda \phi \tag{4.12}$$

Then, according to Eqs. (4.11) and (4.12), the wage of unskilled workers in region r can be expressed as follows:

$$w_r^A = 1 - q_r^A = 1 - \frac{1}{M}(A_r - \lambda_r \phi) \tag{4.13}$$

Based on the above analysis, the wage differential of unskilled workers between the gate region and hinterland can be expressed as follows:

$$w_G^A - w_H^A = \frac{2\phi}{M}\lambda - \frac{\phi}{M} \tag{4.14}$$

We now determine the T and t conditions needed for trade to occur between any two regions at these equilibrium prices. In particular, there will be two-way trade between domestic regions as long as the price of manufacturing p_{rs} can compensate for the transport costs. That is to say, $p_{rs} - t_{rs} \geq 0$ as long as the transport costs are low enough. Using the equilibrium price (4.6), there is trade between the two domestic regions if

$$t_{rs} < t_{trade} = \frac{2a + cL_R T}{2b + cL} \tag{4.15}$$

As discussed in Behrens (2011), decreasing the international trade costs of T may well spur interregional trade within the liberalizing country due to more manufacturing goods being imported from the overseas market. For the same reason, the occurrence of international trade between the gate region and region R means that $p_{GR} - T_{GH} \geq 0$. Furthermore, the local factors should be large enough to supply the traditional sector. We impose the following restrictions:

$$T_{rs} < T_{trade} = \frac{2a}{2b + cL}, \quad A_r > \lambda_r \phi \tag{4.16}$$

4.3 Spatial Equilibrium

As shown in Ottaviano et al. (2002), the indirect utility of skilled workers in region r can be written as follows:

$$V = S_r^M + S_r^A + w_r^M + \bar{q}_0 \tag{4.17}$$

where

$$S_r^M = \frac{a^2 N}{2b} - a \int_0^N p_r(v)dv + \frac{b + cN}{2} \int_0^N [p_r(v)]^2 dv - \frac{c}{2} \left[\int_0^N p_r(v)dv \right]^2 \tag{4.18}$$

is the individual consumption surplus of manufacturing goods, and S_r^A is the corresponding surplus of traditional goods. The skilled workers are mobile between the domestic regions and migrate between them according to the difference in indirect utility levels (ΔV). The consumer's indirect utility differential between the domestic regions can be defined as follows:

$$\Delta V(\lambda) = S_G^M - S_H^M + w_G^M - w_H^M + S_G^A - S_H^A \tag{4.19}$$

Because the access to traditional varieties of goods in each region is same, the differential of surplus in terms of traditional goods (S_r^A) between any two regions is zero. Thus, the indirect utility differential between the two domestic regions can be written as $\Delta V(\lambda) = S_G^M - S_H^M + w_G^M - w_H^M$ for short.

Here, this chapter assumes that the home country and the rest of the world have an identical market size ($L = n_G + n_H = n_R \equiv n$, $N = 2n$, $A_R = A_H + A_G = A$) and that the unskilled workers are evenly distributed between the domestic regions ($A_G = A_H = A/2$). By using Eqs. (4.6), (4.7), and (4.8), the equilibrium price index of the two domestic regions can be written as

$$P_G = \frac{2an + (b+2cn)(n_H t + nT)}{2b+2cn}, P_H = \frac{2an + (b+2cn)(n_G t + nT + nt)}{2b+2cn} \tag{4.20}$$

Based on some straightforward yet cumbersome calculation, we can obtain the differential of consumption surplus for manufacturing goods and the differential of skilled workers' wages between the gate region and the hinterland as follows:

$$S_G^M - S_H^M = \frac{b+2cn}{8\phi_m(b+cn)^2}\left[\left(\alpha_1 t^2 + \alpha_2 t + 4c^2n^3Tt\right)\lambda + \alpha_3 Tt\right] \tag{4.21}$$

$$\alpha_1 = -\left(4b^2n + 8bcn^2\right) < 0 \tag{4.22}$$

$$\alpha_2 = \left(8abn + 16acn^2\right) > 0 \tag{4.23}$$

$$\alpha_3 = -\left[4c^2n^3 + 8bcn^2 + 4b^2n\right] < 0 \tag{4.24}$$

$$w_G^M - w_H^M = \frac{b+2cn}{8\phi_m(b+cn)^2}\left[\left(\zeta_1 t^2 + \zeta_2 t + \zeta_3 Tt\right)\lambda + \psi_1 t + \psi_2 t^2 \psi_3 Tt\right] - \frac{2\phi}{M}\lambda + \frac{\phi}{M} \tag{4.25}$$

$$\zeta_1 = -\left(4c^2n^3 + 4Ac^2n^2 + 4Abcn + 4bcn^2 + 2b^2n\right) < 0 \tag{4.26}$$

$$\zeta_2 = 4abn > 0 \tag{4.27}$$

$$\zeta_3 = 4bcn^2 + 2c^2n^3 > 0 \tag{4.28}$$

$$\psi_1 = 4Aab + 4Aacn > 0 \tag{4.29}$$

$$\psi_2 = -\left(2Ab^2 + 2Abcn\right) < 0 \tag{4.30}$$

$$\psi_3 = -\left(2c^2n^3 + 4bcn^2 + 2Ac^2n^2 + 6Abcn + 2b^2n + 4Ab^2\right) < 0 \tag{4.31}$$

where α_1, α_2, α_3, ζ_1, ζ_2, ζ_3, ψ_1, ψ_2, and ψ_3 are bundles of parameters independent of trade and transport costs.

According to Eqs. (4.21) and (4.22), we can explain where the agglomeration and dispersion forces arise. The agglomeration forces can be observed in the first bracketed term in Eqs. (4.21) and (4.22). When the coefficient of λ is positive, these terms increase in λ. That is, when more skilled workers relocate to the gate region, the skilled workers' wages and net surplus of manufacturing goods will increase correspondingly. To go into more detail, agglomeration forces derive from the home market effects, which are caused by the *demand linkage* and the *cost linkage*.

When more skilled workers agglomerate in the gate region, the larger demand will increase the profits of firms and then improve the wages of skilled workers (see (4.21)). Meanwhile, more firms (skilled workers) agglomerate in the gate region; the fierce competition lowers the price of a variety of goods and increases the consumption surplus of manufacturing (see (4.22)). These agglomeration forces are called the second-nature force and are mentioned in Krugman (1991) and Ottaviano et al. (2002).

Performing another role in the spatial equilibrium, the dispersion forces in our model mainly derive from the product market crowding effect. In addition, unskilled workers that are employed in the manufacturing sector contribute to the spatial configuration as another centrifugal force. Firstly, when the coefficient of λ is negative in the first bracketed terms in (4.21) and (4.22), more skilled workers agglomerate in the gate region, and the skilled workers' wage and the net surplus of manufacturing decrease in λ. Indeed, when more firms agglomerate in the gate region, the fierce competition decreases the price of the products and the skilled workers' wage. In particular, when trade costs T and transport costs t are extremely large, the dispersion forces dominate the economic system. At the same time, when more firms locate in the gate region, the skilled workers' wage decreases in λ, as described in the second term in Eq. (4.22). With more skilled workers locating in the gate region, the larger demand increases the profits of manufacturing firms. Because unskilled workers are employed as fixed costs as well as the skilled workers in the manufacturing sector, the revenue of firms is equal to the wages of the skilled and unskilled workers. The increase of the wage share of unskilled workers extrudes the amount of wage that is allocated to skilled workers. This additional dispersion force derived from the traditional sector has rarely been observed in prior papers, except those of Picard and Zeng (2005, 2010). When we detect the second term of Eq. (4.22), we note that it is independent of trade and transport costs. This means that even with full agglomeration in one region, dispersion could emerge again if the dispersion force increases.

In the equilibrium, the skilled worker never intends to move to another location. When there is a tiny marginal deviation from the equilibrium, the skilled workers still return to the equilibrium state. We call such a state stable equilibrium. Formally, such a stable spatial equilibrium can be expressed by using following (in) equalities:

$$\lambda \in (0,1) \text{ if } \Delta V = 0 \tag{4.32}$$

$$\lambda = 0 \text{ if } \Delta V \leq 0 \tag{4.33}$$

$$\lambda = 1 \text{ if } \Delta V \geq 0 \tag{4.34}$$

Such an equilibrium always occurs because ΔV is a continuous function of λ. The stable equilibrium can be divided into interior and corner equilibriums. An interior equilibrium is stable if and only if the slope of the utility differential

Eq. (4.19) is non-positive in a neighborhood of this equilibrium, whereas a corner equilibrium is stable if $\lambda = 1$ and $\Delta V \geq 0$ or $\lambda = 0$ and $\Delta V \leq 0$.

After substituting (4.21) and (4.22) into (4.19), the differential of indirect utility between the gate region and the hinterland can be written as follows:

$$\Delta V(\lambda) = \left[(\theta_1 t + \theta_2 t^2 + \theta_3 tT - \eta_1)\lambda + (\varphi_1 t + \varphi_2 t^2 + \varphi_3 tT + \eta_2)\right] \tag{4.35}$$

where

$$\theta_1 = \frac{b + 2cn}{8(b + cn)^2}\left(12abn + 16acn^2\right) > 0 \tag{4.36}$$

$$\theta_2 = -\frac{b + 2cn}{8(b + cn)^2}\left(4c^2n^3 + 12bcn^2 + 4Ac^2n^2 + 6b^2n + 4Abcn\right) < 0 \tag{4.37}$$

$$\theta_3 = \frac{b + 2cn}{8(b + cn)^2}\left(4bcn^2 + 6c^2n^3\right) > 0 \tag{4.38}$$

$$\varphi_1 = \frac{b + 2cn}{8(b + cn)^2}(4Aab + 4Aacn) > 0 \tag{4.39}$$

$$\varphi_2 = -\frac{b + 2cn}{8(b + cn)^2}\left(2Ab^2 + 2Abcn\right) < 0 \tag{4.40}$$

$$\varphi_3 = -\frac{b + 2cn}{8(b + cn)^2}\left(6c^2n^3 + 12bcn^2 + 2Ac^2n^2 + 6Abcn + 6b^2n + 4Ab^2\right) < 0 \tag{4.41}$$

$$\eta_1 = \frac{8(b + cn)^2}{b + 2cn}\frac{2\phi}{M} \tag{4.42}$$

$$\eta_2 = \frac{8(b + cn)^2}{b + 2cn}\frac{\phi}{M} \tag{4.43}$$

are bundles of constant parameters. Thus the differential of indirect utility between the two domestic regions depends only on the two exogenous variables, transport costs, t, and trade costs, T. We note that the utility differential is a simple linear function of λ.

Following the above-mentioned discussion, the distribution of skilled workers in the home country can be shown as follows. According to Eqs. (4.23), (4.24), and (4.25), the agglomeration of skilled workers in the gate region is a stable equilibrium if and only if $\Delta V(1) > 0$. This means that the differential of utility in the gate region is larger than that in the hinterland. Some straightforward calculations tell us that $\Delta V(\lambda = 1) \geq 0$ is equivalent to:

$$\Delta V = (\theta_2 + \varphi_2)t^2 + [\theta_1 + \varphi_1 + (\theta_3 + \varphi_3)T]t - \eta > 0 \tag{4.44}$$

where

$$\theta_1 + \varphi_1 = \frac{b + 2cn}{8(b + cn)^2}\left(12abn + 16acn^2 + 4Aab + 4Aacn\right) > 0 \tag{4.45}$$

$$\theta_2 + \varphi_2 = -\frac{b + 2cn}{8(b + cn)^2}\left(4c^2n^3 + 12bc^2n^2 + 4Ac^2n^2 + 6b^2n + 6Abcn + 2Ab^2\right) < 0 \tag{4.46}$$

$$\theta_3 + \varphi_3 = -\frac{b + 2cn}{8(b + cn)^2}\left(8bcn^2 + 2Ac^2n^2 + 6Abcn + 6b^2n + 4Ab^2\right) < 0 \tag{4.47}$$

$$\eta = \frac{8(b + cn)^2}{b + 2cn}\frac{\phi}{M} \tag{4.48}$$

are parameters independent of transport and trade costs. If we write $F(t,T) = (\theta_2 + \varphi_2)t^2 + [\theta_1 + \varphi_1 + (\theta_3 + \varphi_3)T]t - \eta$, the foregoing condition can be written as $F(t,T) \geq 0$. Similarly, $\lambda = 0$ is also a stable equilibrium if and only if $\Delta V(0) \leq 0$. The full agglomeration in the hinterland means that skilled workers enjoy a lower indirect utility in the gate region. This is equivalent to $\Delta V(\lambda = 0) = \varphi_2 t^2 + (\varphi_1 + \varphi_3 T)t + \eta < 0$. If we write $G(t,T) = \varphi_2 t^2 + (\varphi_1 + \varphi_3 T)t + \eta_2$, we can have $G(t,T) < 0$.

Finally, $\lambda \in (0,1)$ is an interior stable equilibrium if and only if $\Delta V(\lambda) = 0$ and the coefficient of λ is negative in (4.26). For skilled workers, there is no incentive to move to another location. Because $\Delta V = [(\theta_1 t + \theta_2 t^2 + \theta_3 tT - \eta_1)\lambda + (\varphi_1 t + \varphi_2 t^2 + \varphi_3 tT + \eta_2)]$, these two conditions for the interior stable equilibrium show that $\lambda = \frac{G(t,T)}{-H(t,T)} \in (0,1)$ and $H(t,T) < 0$, where $H(t,T) = \theta_1 t + \theta_2 t^2 + \theta_3 tT - \eta_1$. This means that this condition is equal to $G(t,T) > 0$ and $G(t,T) + H(t,T) < 0$. Also, because $F(t,T) = G(t,T) + H(t,T)$, the foregoing conditions of spatial equilibrium, (4.23), (4.24), and (4.25), can be rewritten as follows:

$$\lambda = 1 \text{ if } F(t,T) \geq 0 \tag{4.49}$$

$$\lambda = 0 \text{ if } G(t,T) < 0 \tag{4.50}$$

$$\lambda \in (0,1) \text{if } G(t,T) > 0 \text{ and } F(t,T) < 0 \tag{4.51}$$

Based on the above discussion, we then study the impacts of the asymmetrical geographical access on the national equilibrium during the trade liberalization and regional integration.

4.4 The Effects of Trade Liberalization and Regional Integration

Because $F(t,T)$ and $G(t,T)$ are functions of t and T, this allows us to investigate how international trade liberalization and regional integration affect the distribution of manufacturing firms in the home country. For the sake of simplicity, the aim of this chapter is to focus on how regional integration may affect the equilibrium distribution of manufacturing firms in the country by assuming differentiated international trade environments. In other words, we concentrate on the analysis of domestic transport cost t by assuming international trade cost T to be a series of different values. In addition, $F(t,T)$ and $G(t,T)$ are quadratic function of t. When $F(t,T)$ and $G(t,T)$ are put in the same coordinate system, we find that the relationship between $F(t,T)$ and $G(t,T)$ mainly depends on the locations of their corresponding symmetric axes, which are also related to T. Here, we denote the symmetric axes of quadratic functions $F(t,T)$ and $G(t,T)$ to be t_F and t_G, respectively. Thus, we can write $t_F = \frac{\theta_1+\varphi_1+(\theta_3+\varphi_3)T}{-2(\theta_2+\varphi_2)}$ and $t_G = \frac{\varphi_1+\varphi_3 T}{-2\varphi_2}$, which can be expressed as two lines in the plane of (T,t). If we compare the slopes and intercepts of the two lines, we can write $\frac{\theta_3+\varphi_3}{-2(\theta_2+\varphi_2)} > \frac{\varphi_3}{-2\varphi_2}$ and $\frac{\theta_1+\varphi_1}{-2(\theta_2+\varphi_2)} < \frac{\varphi_1}{-2\varphi_2}$ according to the signs of the parameters in (4.26). Then, we can show these two lines in the following figure.

As can be seen from Fig. 4.2, When $t_F = t_G$, $t_G = 0$, and $t_F = 0$, we can obtain T^*, T_1, and T_2, respectively. The three points divide the horizontal axis into four intervals, i.e.,$[0,T^*]$,$[T^*,T_1]$, $[T_1,T_2]$, and $[T_2,T_{trade})$. In the following discussion, we mainly focus on two cases: when international trade costs are very high and when they are very low, i.e., $T \in [0,T^*]$ and $[T_2,T_{trade})$. The discussion of the other two cases, i.e., $T \in [T^*,T_1]$ and $[T_1,T_2]$ is given in Appendix B. The two cases to be discussed here are concerned with the following two regional integrations.

Fig. 4.2 The relationship between t_F and t_G

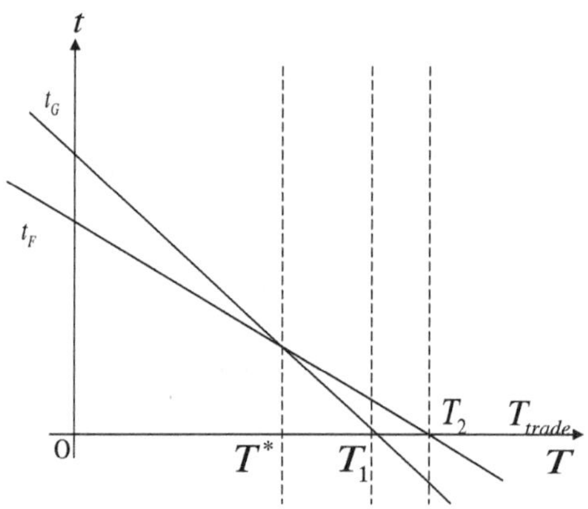

4.4.1 *Regional Integration When a Country Is Closed to Global Markets*

We first investigate the impacts of domestic regional integration on countries that are endowed with relatively closed international trade environments. To do so, we assume that the international trade costs are sufficiently high, i.e., $T \in [T_2, T_{trade})$. As shown in Fig. 4.2, when T is in $[T_2, T_{trade})$, t_F and t_G have negative values of t simultaneously. This means that the symmetrical axis of quadratic curves $F(t, T)$ and $G(t, T)$ both lie on left side of the plane of $(t, \Delta V)$. We can then depict them in the following figure, which involves the relationship between $F(t, T)$ and $G(t, T)$. As Fig. (4.3a) shows, when $t \in [t_4, t_{trade})$, we can see that $G(t, T) < 0$. This means that $\Delta V < 0$, and thus, $\lambda = 0$ according to (4.29). When $\lambda = 0$, this means all the firms agglomerate in the hinterland. Following closely, in the interval $[0, t_4]$, we can see that $G(t, T) > 0$ and $F(t, T) < 0$ in Fig. (4.3a). Thus, we have $\lambda \in (0, 1)$ according to Eq. (4.30). Because function $\lambda(t) = G(t)/-H(t)$ is a monotonic and continuous function of t and the endpoints are $\lambda(0) = 1/2$ and $\lambda(t_4) = 0$, we then know that when $t \in [0, t_4]$, this interior solution λ is larger than 0 and smaller than $1/2$. Based on the foregoing discussion, the relationship can be drawn in Fig. (4.3b), and the aforementioned results can be summarized as follows.

Consider a country with two asymmetrical domestic regions and very high international trade costs, i.e., $T \in [T_2, T_{trade})$. When interregional transport costs, t, are extremely high, all manufacturing firms will locate in the hinterland so as to avoid competition from rest of the world. When transport costs decrease considerably, firms will move from the hinterland to the gate region until an even distribution is reached.

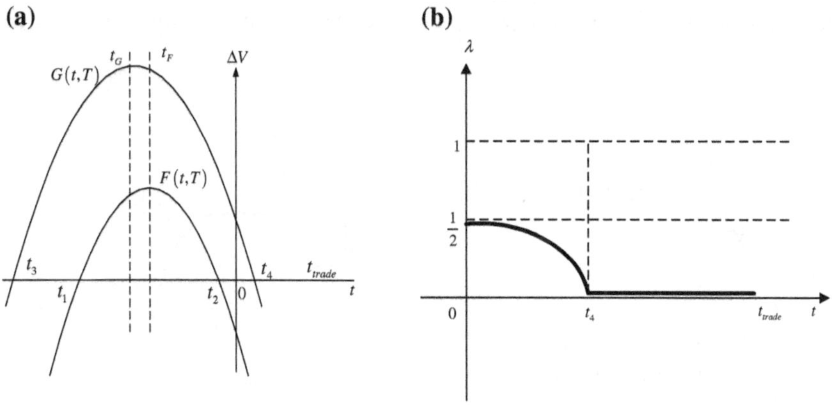

Fig. 4.3 Industry location when T is very high

4.4.2 Regional Integration When a Country Is Open to Global Markets

In contrast to the previous subsection, here, we attempt to investigate the effects of regional integration on the space economy in a home country characterized by advantageous international trade environments. This implies that international trade costs are extremely low, i.e., $T \in [0, T^*]$ and that there is a large volume of trade between the home country and global markets. As can be seen from Fig. 4.2, when $T \in [0, T^*]$, t_G and t_F are both positive, and t_G is located on the right side of t_F. In addition, when $t_G > t_F$, it can be verified that the larger roots of equation $F(t, T)=0$ are larger than those of $G(t, T)=0$ (see Appendix C). In this circumstance, we can show an explicit relationship between ΔV and t in Fig. (4.4a). When $t \in [t_4, t_{trade})$, we know that $G(t, T) < 0$, as shown in Fig. (4.4a). As argued in the previous subsection, we can have $\lambda = 0$ according to Eq. (4.29). As transport costs gradually decrease, when $t \in [t_2, t_4]$, we can see that $G(t, T) > 0$ and $F(t, T) < 0$, as shown in Fig. (4.4a). This then implies that $0 < \lambda < 1$ based on (4.30). When t surpasses t_2, there exists an interval $[t_1, t_2]$, and we can obtain $F(t, T) > 0$ from Fig. (4.4a). As can be seen from (4.28), we now have $\lambda = 1$. With the further decrease of transport costs, Fig. (4.4a) tells us that $G(t, T) > 0$ and $F(t, T) < 0$ when $t \in [0, t_1]$. As occurred in the interval of $[t_2, t_4]$, this satisfies the condition of $0 < \lambda < 1$ in accordance with (4.30). Here, as discussed in the foregoing subsection, $\lambda(t)$ is a monotonic and continuous function of t, and the endpoints are $\lambda(0) = 1/2$ and $\lambda(t_1) = 0$. We then know that when $t \in [0, t_1]$, this interior solution λ is larger than $1/2$ and smaller than 1. To sum up, the relationship between λ and t is illustrated in Fig. (4.4b).

Based on the foregoing discussion, we can summarize that when the home country is open to global markets, i.e.,$T \in [0, T^*]$, the migration of the home country adopts several spatial patterns. When transport costs are high, similar to the situation described in Subsection 4.1, when the trade costs are high, all firms will

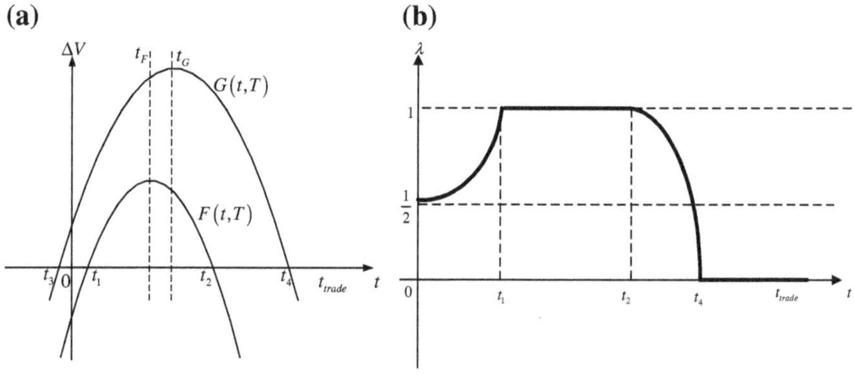

Fig. 4.4 Industrial location when T is very low

locate in the hinterland. The gradual decrease in transport costs will trigger the firms to move to the gate region, where they can save on the trade costs for exporting goods to global markets. There is an interval, i.e.,$[t_1, t_2]$, in which a full agglomeration in the gate region will happen during the regional integration. With further decreases in transport costs, firms will relocate again and move from the gate region to the hinterland, where the wage of unskilled workers is lower. Eventually, an even distribution of firms between the two regions occurs.

4.4.3 Interpretation and Discussion

The aforementioned analytical results show the impacts of regional integration and trade liberalization on the space economy of the home country. Firstly, when trade costs are sufficiently high, the spatial economy has a full agglomeration of industries in the hinterland and then experiences a process of dispersion until an even industrial distribution between the two domestic regions occurs during regional integration. Secondly, when trade costs are very low and transport costs are high, industrial firms will first concentrate in the hinterland, but a decrease in transport costs will trigger a relocation of firms from the hinterland to the gate region until a full agglomeration occurs in the gate region, which will be sustained for a good while. With a further decrease in transport costs, regional integration will result in an even spatial distribution of firms between the two regions. In our model, the domestic regions are endowed with asymmetric accessibility to the external world market, which reflects the reality in many countries, such as Mexico and China. This allows us to give a more realistic explanation for the spatial evolution in many developing countries. As shown in Krugman and Livas (1996), high trade costs caused manufacturing firms to concentrate in the Mexico City region, which is far away from the US-Mexico border. However, during the rapid trade liberalization, a large share of industry relocated to the US border region. Meanwhile, Gallup et al. (1999) find that when domestic regions are poorly integrated, the population is agglomerated in the hinterland rather than in the coastal areas. This is supported by the fact that a greater share of the people live away from coastal regions in Sub-Saharan African. This chapter's analytical results also show how industrial firms are relocated to the gate region. In this way, as Fujita and Hu (2001) point out, economic development in China has caused a strong agglomeration toward the coastal regions. This can be attributed to the fact that the coastal regions in China are endowed with better accessibility for exporting goods to global markets. The asymmetric considerations in our model not only explain why economic agglomeration occurs but also show where agglomeration arises.

In the literature, asymmetry in terms of accessibility has been employed in other recent papers (Crozet and Koenig 2004; Behrens et al. 2006a). Unlike Crozet and Koenig (2004), we successfully show the analytical results. Moreover, international trade costs and interregional transport costs are considered simultaneously in order to investigate their impacts on the space economy of a country. In the present model, skilled workers and unskilled workers are both hired in the manufacturing sector. The employment of unskilled workers in manufacturing firms constitutes another dispersion force that generates redispersion during economic integration. In Behrens et al. (2006a), firms would always concentrate in the gate region when the domestic regions were well-integrated, but they failed to show industrial redispersion. Concerning industrial redispersion, since Williamson (1965), reasons behind the disparity between regions (countries) in terms of divergence and convergence have always been debated. During the initial period of industrialization, manufacturing firms tend to agglomerate in some special regions or major cities and then experience a process of deconcentration. In Brazil, some industries have relocated from the metropolitan areas of Sao Paulo and Rio de Janeiro to the adjacent areas of Santa Catarina and Minas Gerais, as discussed by Haddad and Peroblli (2003a, 2003b). Even in some small countries, such as South Korea, Kwon (1985) pointed out that plants relocated from the core metro areas of Seoul, Pusan, and Taegu and their satellite cities to the rest of the country. The impetus for this deconcentration is mainly derived from the improvement in infrastructure and economic liberalization that occurred after the 1970s in South Korea. In China, the growth rate of per capita GDP exhibited some convergence between the late 1990s and 2006, when there was a large gap between the hinterland and coastal regions (Fan and Sun 2008). This recent empirical evidence suggests that the improvements in transport infrastructure have effects in terms of attracting industries to periphery regions or hinterlands.

In previous papers, the process of industrial redispersion has been obtained by using urban costs and various investment mechanisms (Tabuchi 1998; Tabuchi and Thisse 2002). In the real world, the dispersion forces generated from the employment of unskilled workers seem to be more widely observed in developing countries. Picard and Zeng (2005) investigated the process of industrial redispersion by considering the agricultural sector and a different production function. Compared with their symmetrical two-region model, our model also takes into account the considerations of asymmetry in terms of accessibility. The results obtained in our paper seem to approach nearer to the real economy. The previous models of industrial redispersion offer reasonable mechanisms to explain the occurrence of industrial deconcentration, but their weak point is that they fail to describe where the agglomeration occurs and where the deconcentration comes from. In China, during the past three decades, the eastern coastal provinces, with better accessibility for exporting goods, have dominated the inlands and become the core region during economic liberalization and development. Moreover, in the past ten years, industrial redispersion has been observed. Our model not only gives an explanation of where the industrial agglomeration occurs but also where the redispersion comes from by considering asymmetrical regions.

4.5 Concluding Remarks

The importance of geography itself has always been ignored in the previous NEG studies designed to investigate industrial location during economic integration. Despite the attention given to the role of market access in shaping the landscape of the economy in developed countries, little concern is paid to developing countries, particularly in the field of theoretical work. In this chapter, it is assumed that the hinterland must go through the gate region to access to overseas markets, and the rest of the world is considered to be an overseas market. To better reveal the current situation in developing countries, this book assumed that unskilled workers are employed both in the manufacturing sector and the traditional sector, as did in Forslid and Ottaviano (2003). As a result, industrial redispersion was analytically derived within our framework.

This book found that when the home country is closed to overseas markets, the high interregional transport costs allow the hinterland to attract all of manufacturing firms. However, with the sufficient integration of the domestic economy, there will be a balanced distribution of industry between the gate region and the hinterland. When the home country is open enough to world markets, the firms initially agglomerate in the hinterland and then gradually move to the gate region until a full concentration occurs during the integration of the domestic regions. With further regional economic integration, half of firms will relocate to the hinterland again, with the other half of them remaining in the gate region. Thus, industrial redispersion occurs.

Appendix 1: Discussion of Other Two Cases

1.1 $[T^* < T < T_1]$: We know that $t_F > t_G > 0$ according to the analysis in Fig. 4.2. The possible relationship between differential of indirect utility and transport costs and the corresponding industrial patterns are depicted in Fig. 4.5. Starting from full agglomeration in the hinterland, a gradual decrease in transport cost t causes the industrial firms to catastrophically (or gradually) move to the gate region and remain in a symmetric distribution between the two regions eventually.

1.2 $[T_1 < T < T_2]$: In Fig. 4.2, we know that $t_F > 0$ and $t_G < 0$. There are two possible relationships between $F(t)$ and $G(t)$ when their symmetrical axes are fixed, which is shown in Fig. 4.6. In this case, full agglomeration is the main location pattern. The agglomeration of firms first occurs in the hinterland and then either in the hinterland or the gate region. However, further decreases in interregional transport costs trigger the gradual symmetric distribution of industrial firms between the two domestic regions.

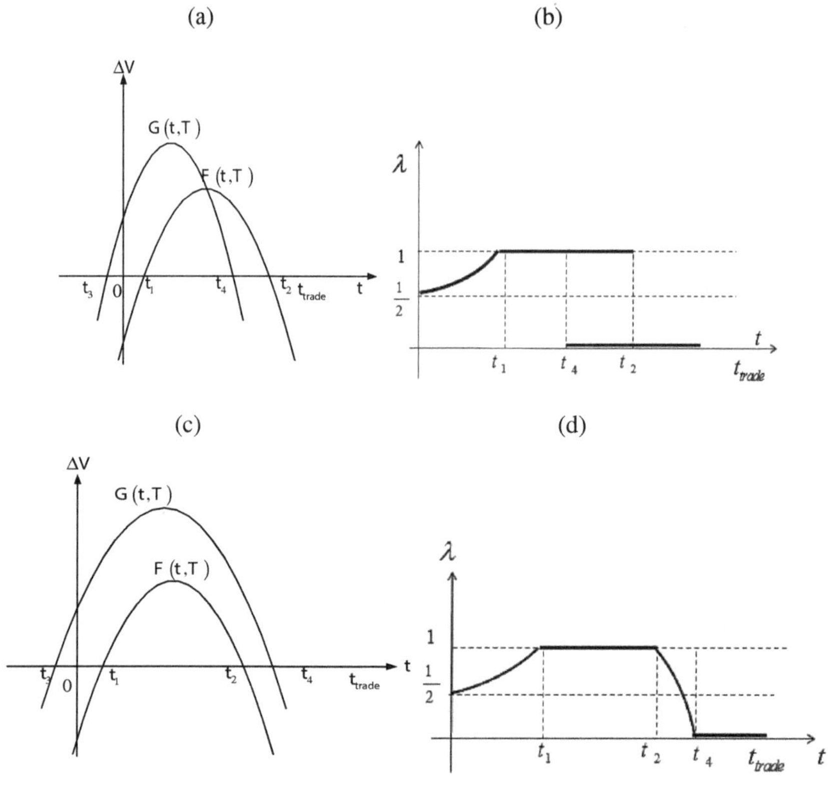

Fig. 4.5 Industry location and interregional transport costs

Appendix 2: Proof

We can write $F(t){=}at^2+bt-\eta$ and $G(t,T){=}a^{'}t^2+b^{'}t+\eta$, where $a=(\theta_2+\varphi_2){<}0,b=\theta_1+\varphi_1+(\theta_3+\varphi_3)T>0;a^{'}=\varphi_2{<}0,b^{'}=\varphi_1+\varphi_3T>0$, and $\eta>0$. The larger root values of $F(t){=}0$ and $G(t){=}0$ can be written as $t_2^F=\frac{b+\sqrt{b^2+4a\eta}}{-2a}$ and $t_2^G=\frac{b^{'}+\sqrt{b^{'2}-4a^{'}\eta}}{-2a^{'}}$, respectively.

Thus,

$$\begin{aligned} t_2^G-t_2^F &= \left(\frac{b^{'}}{-2a^{'}}+\frac{\sqrt{b^{'2}-4a^{'}\eta}}{-2a^{'}}\right)-\left(\frac{b}{-2a}+\frac{\sqrt{b^2+4a\eta}}{-2a}\right) \\ &= \left(\frac{b^{'}}{-2a^{'}}-\frac{b}{-2a}\right)+\left(\frac{\sqrt{b^{'2}-4a^{'}\eta}}{-2a^{'}}-\frac{\sqrt{b^2+4a\eta}}{-2a}\right) \end{aligned} \tag{4.52}$$

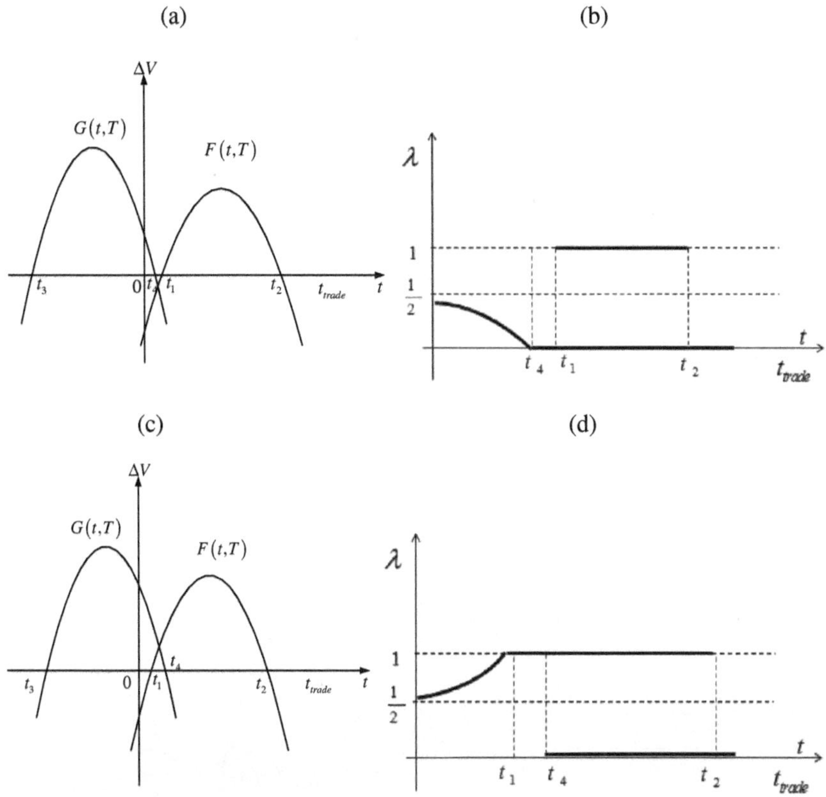

Fig. 4.6 Industry location and interregional transport costs

During the interval of $[0, T^*]$, s_G is larger than s_F, as shown in Fig. 4.5. This means that the symmetrical axis of $G(t)$ is located on the right side of $F(t)$ and that $\frac{b'}{-2a'} > \frac{b}{-2a}$ for equations $F(t){=}0$ and $G(t){=}0$. We then know that the first term in (4.52) is positive. In addition, $\left(\frac{\sqrt{b'^2-4a'\eta}}{-2a'}\right)^2 - \left(\frac{\sqrt{b^2+4a\eta}}{-2a}\right)^2 = \frac{b'^2-4a'\eta}{4a'^2} - \frac{b^2+4a\eta}{4a^2}$ $= \frac{b'^2}{4a'^2} - \frac{b^2}{4a^2} - \left(\frac{a+a'}{a'a}\right)\eta$. Noting that $\frac{b'}{-2a'} > \frac{b}{-2a} > 0$, $a<0, a'<0$, and $\eta > 0$, it is readily verifiable that $\frac{b'^2}{4a'^2} - \frac{b^2}{4a^2} - \left(\frac{a+a'}{a'a}\right)\eta > 0$. Then, we can deduce that the second term in (4.52) is also positive. It is equivalent to $t_2^G > t_2^F$. Additionally, when $t = 0$, $F(t) < 0$, and $G(t) > 0$, we are able to depict the parabolas of functions $F(t)$ and $G(t)$ in the same coordinate axis, as shown in Fig. 4.2.

Chapter 5
Empirical Investigation of Home Market Effect: New Evidence from China

5.1 Introduction

Spatial economics, also called new trade theory (NTT) and new economic geography (NEG), has made much progress in trade theory and economic geography over the past three decades. Following Krugman's seminal papers (Krugman 1980, 1991), countless refinements and rapid progress (Helpman and Krugman 1985; Martin and Rogers 1995; Ottaviano et al. 2002; Forslid and Ottaviano 2003; Pflüger 2004) have been made in investigating space-economy in terms of trade pattern and the geographic location of economic activities. To a large extent, spatial economics has entered a mature phase. However, spatial economics still has some internal and external drawbacks and challenges. The striking feature is the paradox between the maturity of the theoretical model and the unsettled state of empirical research, which remains unsettled in both methodology and results. As argued in Head and Mayer (2004), there is no agreed regression to estimate, nor even a consensus dependent variable to explain.

Given the foregoing, the models of spatial economics mainly consist of NTT and NEG elements. It should be clear that these two models are closely related and share the same conceptual framework, that is, the home market effect (HME). As a building block of spatial economics, HME is always considered the basis of NTT and NEG. Theoretical results (Krugman 1980; Behrens et al. 2009; Takahashi et al. 2013; Zeng and Uchikawa 2014) also indicate that it is sound and robust. Unfortunately, researchers seldom investigate the workings of HME empirically. Among the reasons for the slow progress in testing HME is primarily the unsettled state of its basic definition. As noted by Takahashi et al. (2013), the theoretical basis of HME is still under construction. Krugman (1980) initiates the literature by demonstrating that a country with a relatively large local demand will run a trade surplus. Further, Helpman and Krugman (1985, Sect. 10.4) show that the larger local demand attracts a more-than-proportionate share of firms. In terms of factor price, Krugman (1991, p. 91) defines HME as the fact that, other things being equal,

J. Wang, *Economic Analysis of Industrial Agglomeration*,
https://doi.org/10.1007/978-981-10-7437-0_5

wages are higher in larger regions. The definition of HME can be interpreted from three different standpoints.

Definitions vary from one study to the next, but most empirical studies testing HME focus mainly on investigating firm shares and exports. As primary empirical writers on HME, Davis and Weinstein (1999, 2003) investigate the existence of HME by simultaneously considering comparative advantage. The approach that they take in their work allows them to distinguish traditional trade theory from NTT. By employing data from Japan and OECD, they produce results which have the effect of supporting HME. Head and Ries (2001) study HME with data from North America and obtain their results through cross-industry data and corresponding industry over time. Reviewing the related papers on testing HME, we find that these studies mainly set out to investigate the magnification effect between production, export, and local demand. But so far, there has been no entirely conclusive test of HME. Unlike tests of the effect of market potential on factor price (Hanson 2005; Redding and Venables 2004; Head and Mayer 2006; Hering and Poncet 2010), the results of testing HME are not always consistent with each other. In Davis and Weinstein (1999), the pooled results tell us that after controlling factors (comparative advantage), the coefficients of IDIODEM (HME) are all less than one. In line with the authors' intentions, the results do not imply that HME must exist. As argued by Head and Mayer (2004), the pooled results of Davis and Weinstein (1999) offer only confirmation of the presence or absence of HME. As another strand, the results of Head and Ries (2001) also vary in relation to their use of different data. The data in terms of cross-industry and over time finally give different coefficients in different dimensions. These related studies then have not given us unitary responses. The fundamental problem arise the HME still remains to be defined. In terms of testing HME, which considerations should be given?

First of all, transport costs as essential ingredients of spatial economics are always absent from the related empirical studies. Pure theoretical models tell us that HME is robust and sound, but transport costs should imperatively be included in these outcomes. Without trade costs, markets are not segmented, and without market segmentation firm location is irrelevant (Behrens and Roert-Nicoud 2009). If we consider HME as a magnification effect, it is closely related to transport costs. Through the empirics of HME, we find that some results even reverse the magnification effect. Head and Mayer (2004) also illustrate that a non-monotonic relationship between HME and trade barriers occurs when the elasticity of the labor supply changes. Indeed, HME itself is magnified by declining trade costs (Head and Ries 2001). To avoid confusion with the magnification effect, as suggested by Head and Mayer (2004), this kind of magnification can also be called the "secondary magnification effect" (SME).

Furthermore, SME does not always bring a positive effect. With further decreases in transport costs, the reverse situation even occurs. This means that there is a nonmonotonic relationship between firm share (or factor price) and transport costs. The underlying intuition is that when transport costs fall, some firms will relocate from the core to the periphery, and industrial re-dispersion occurs. Whether NEG models or NTT theoretical models, they all reveal that agglomeration is not the final state of further trade liberalization. Various papers attempt to demonstrate this industrial redispersion by considering urban costs (Tabuchi 1998; Helpman 1998; Ottaviano et al. 2002; Takatsuka and Zeng 2009), housing sector (Suedekum 2006), heterogeneous preference (Tabuchi and Thisse 2002), the immobility of workers with input–output linkages (Venables 1996; Puga 1999), the positive transport costs for traditional goods (Fujita et al. 1999; Picard and Zeng 2005), multiple industries with differentiated labor intensiveness (Zeng 2006), the use of land for production (Pflüger and Tabuchi 2010), and comparative advantage (Picard and Zeng 2010). In contrast to the core—periphery pattern in spatial economics, industrial re-dispersion or decentralization could be considered with another equilibrium result.

It is worth clarifying that the related empirical studies in terms of HME mainly concentrate on investigating the relationship between firm share and local demand. It seems that little attention has been paid to investigating the dimension of factor price (wages). The reasons for ignoring wages are that the related theoretical models in terms of HME heavily rely on employing labor as the only production factor (Krugman 1980; Helpman and Krugman 1985; Behrens et al. 2009). Moreover, the agricultural sector[1] is added to allow for the reaction in production to demand in the increasing return to scale. Since labor is employed by the agricultural sector as the only input, the factor price, wages (the price factor) are equalized between the two regions. Due to this specific assumption, the HME in terms of firm location can be observed, but HME in terms of wages cannot be demonstrated. Additionally, as another strand of refinement for spatial economics, the quasi-linear preference is employed, and an analytical result is successfully obtained in Ottaviano et al. (2002). Since it is assumed to be quasi-linear, the level of capital returns has no impact on the demand for the manufactured good and none in turn on the inter-regional firm distribution. Obviating this problem, when the economy is assumed to have one sector, wages will differ between regions. It is worth mentioning that even with a CES utility, Takahashi et al. (2013) demonstrate the equivalence of a spatial disparity in firm share and in wages by revisiting the HME with the assumption of only one manufacturing sector. Moreover, it can be shown that these spatial inequalities are closely related to transport costs. When transport costs decrease further, an inverted U-shaped pattern of industrial location and wages differential exists. However, this non-monotonic magnification effect is seldom investigated in the empirics of spatial economics. Based on the two-region scenario, Zeng and Uchikawa (2014) generalize the results of Takahashi et al. (2013) into an economic space of multiple regions. Even in multiple regions, wages inequality between any two regions also forms a non-monotonic curve in regions which are more integrated. To sum up, it is almost two decades since the birth of HME. Although many theoretical models claim the existence of various HMEs, these results rely heavily on their specific assumptions. In addition, different empirical studies cannot reach a

[1]The agricultural sector is assumed to exhibit a constant return to scale, perfect competition, homogeneity of goods, and zero transport costs.

consensus either about any definition of or conclusion about HME. Specifically, most empirical works regard the primary magnification effect as the definition of the HME, and the SME is always neglected. Zeng (2014) gives a detailed discussion of the HME and shows that when some specific assumptions are removed, the primary magnification effect is not equivalent to HME in terms of firm share.

In this chapter, we reinvestigate HME in terms of wages and study the evolution of spatial disparity during regional integration. Apart from Davis and Weinstein (1999), most papers choose to empirically examine HME in international cases. However, the subunits of a country can also yield insight into HME, and it is conceivable that HME influences the spatial disparity across regions within a country. Since the transport costs between regions are lower than those at the international level, regional integration could strengthen the effect of secondary magnification on the evolution of spatial economics. Nowadays, globalization has led to an increase in outsourcing in manufacturing, which has spread out from the developed to the developing world. Those who investigate the space-economy within these emerging countries, China in particular finds that the spatial economy is highly reminiscent of the space-economy of advanced countries around 1900 (Krugman 2011). Empirical evidence reveals that the increasing regional disparity in China can be attributed to economic liberalization and globalization between 1985 and 1994 (Fujita and Hu 2001). The evolution of the space-economy in developing countries offers another opportunity to verify the framework of HME. Throughout this chapter, we remain close to the theoretical framework and attempt to interpret a definition of HME. It is found that, over the past few decades, the larger coastal provinces of China have workers and staff in urban units who earn a higher average wages than their counterparts in the interior provinces. Moreover, when transport costs decline further, the disparity in terms of relative wages between the coast and the interior presents a non-monotonic pattern.

The remainder of this chapter is organized as follows. Section 5.2 presents the theoretical framework from which the econometric specifications used in the subsequent sections are derived. In Sect. 5.3, we describe the stylized facts of HME in terms of wages in China. Section 5.4 discusses the related issues of empirical equations and investigates the SME by using data from the level of the Chinese provinces. Section 5.5 concludes the paper.

5.2 Theoretical Framework

In this section, we present a theoretical model to show how the spatial distribution of regional demand affects wages in the model of monopolistic competition and trade. We derive our estimating equation following Takahashi et al. (2013). The spatial economy consists of two regions $\eta = i, j$, which have the same conditions except for their population size. Region i is the larger of the two in terms of population. There are L people in the whole country and the labor endowment in region i is denoted by $\theta\,(1/2 \leq \theta \leq 1)$. There are K units of capital equally owned by L individuals. Unlike the existing studies, this one assumes only one manufacturing sector, having a continuum of varieties. A consumer gains utility only from the manufacturing sector, whose production is under a technology of increasing returns to scale. The utility in the larger region i is

$$U_i = \left[\int_0^N d_n(v)^{\frac{\sigma-1}{\sigma}} di\right]^{\frac{\sigma}{\sigma-1}}, \tag{5.1}$$

where $\sigma > 1$ means a constant elasticity of substitution between any two manufacturing varieties. N is the number of varieties, and $d_i(v)$ is the demand for a manufacturing good v in the larger region i. Since the varieties are symmetrical, the name of the variety will be simplified to d_i to indicate the demand for each variety.

Under the assumption of having only one sector in our economy, the maximization of the consumer's utility function gives the demand in region i for a manufactured good made in region η as ollows:

$$d_{\eta i} = \frac{p_{\eta i}^{-\sigma}}{P_i^{1-\sigma}} Y_i, \ \eta = i, j, \tag{5.2}$$

where Y_i is the income of region i, and $p_{\eta i}$ is the price of a variety produced in region η and sold in region i. Finally, P_i is the price index of manufactured goods in region i which can be written as $P_i = \left[\int_0^N p_i(v)^{1-\sigma} dv\right]^{\frac{1}{1-\sigma}}$, where $p_i(v)$ is the price of variety v sold in region i.

The iceberg transport costs assume that if one unit is shipped from a region only a fraction of it $(1/\tau)$ arrives. In addition, the capital share employed in region i is given by k.

For the production side of the economy, each manufacturing firm has a unit fixed requirement of capital and a marginal input of labor equal to $(\sigma - 1)/\sigma$. Since one firm employs one unit of capital, the total number of firms is equal to the total amount of capital. A firm chooses its optimal inputs so as to maximize its profit, denoted as follows:

$$\pi_i = p_{ii} d_{ii} + p_{ij} d_{ij} - \frac{\sigma - 1}{\sigma} w_i \left(d_{ii} + \tau d_{ij}\right) - r_i, \tag{5.3}$$

where r_i is the capital rent in region i. When we choose the labor in region j as the numéraire, we denote $w_j = 1$ and $w_i = w$. The first-order condition to maximize (5.3) gives $p_{ii} = w$ and $p_{ij} = \tau w$. Similarly, we have $p_{jj} = 1$ and $p_{ji} = \tau$. The price index in two regions can then be written as

$$P_i = \left\{\left[kw^{1-\sigma} + T(1-k)K\right]\right\}^{\frac{1}{1-\sigma}}, \ P_j = \left\{\left[Tw^{1-\sigma}k + (1-k)K\right]\right\}^{\frac{1}{1-\sigma}}, \tag{5.4}$$

where $T = \tau^{1-\sigma} \in (0, 1)$ is trade freedom. Since $\sigma > 1$, greater trade freedom corresponds to a small transport cost.

By the free-entry condition of firms, the zero profit implies that the capital rents in the two regions are as follows:

$$r_i = \frac{1}{\sigma K}\left[\frac{w^{1-\sigma}Y_i}{w^{1-\sigma}k + T(1-k)} + T\frac{w^{1-\sigma}Y_j}{Tw^{1-\sigma}k + 1 - k}\right], \quad r_j = \frac{1}{\sigma K}\left[T\frac{Y_i}{w^{1-\sigma}k + T(1-k)} + T\frac{Y_j}{Tw^{1-\sigma}k + 1 - k}\right] \tag{5.5}$$

Then, the nominal incomes in the two regions are

$$Y_i = \theta K\left[kr_i + (1-k)r_j\right] + \theta wL, \quad Y_j = (1-\theta)K\left[kr_i + (1-k)r_j\right] + (1-\theta)L. \tag{5.6}$$

Since capital is mobile, firms choose their location by a balance of market size and wages rate. We have only interior equilibrium, in which $r_i = r_j = r$. Given this condition, we can obtain income and capital rent in these two regions

$$Y_i = \frac{\theta L[\sigma w + (1-\theta)(1-w)]}{\sigma - 1}, \quad Y_j = \frac{(1-\theta)L[\sigma - \theta(1-w)]}{\sigma - 1}, \tag{5.7}$$

$$r_i = r_j = \frac{L(\theta w + 1 - \theta)}{K(\sigma - 1)} = r. \tag{5.8}$$

In the labor markets, the labor demand in region i is equal to the total labor costs of firms there. According to the foregoing income equation, we can have:

$$k\frac{\sigma - 1}{\sigma}(Y_i + Y_j) = k(\theta w + 1 - \theta)L. \tag{5.9}$$

The labor balance of supply equaling demand gives the simple relationship between wages and firm share:

$$k = \frac{\theta w}{\theta w + 1 - \theta}. \tag{5.10}$$

In addition, we can endogenously obtain the wages. Since the production of each firm in region i is $d_{ii} + \tau d_{ij}$ and the marginal cost in each firm is $(\sigma - 1)/\sigma$, the market-clearing condition of labor in region i can be written as:

$$\theta L = \frac{\sigma - 1}{\sigma} kK(d_{ii} + \tau d_{ij}). \tag{5.11}$$

By using (5.2),(5.4),(5.7) and (5.10), (5.11) yields the following wages equation:

$$\Psi(w) = \Phi_1(w) + \Phi_2(w)T + \Phi_3(w)T^2 = 0, \tag{5.12}$$

where

$$\begin{aligned}\Phi_1(w) =& (w-1)\theta(1-\theta)\\ \Phi_2(w) =& w^{2-\sigma}\left[(1-\theta)w^{2\sigma-3}-\theta\right]\sigma\\ \Phi_3(w) =& \theta(\sigma-1+\theta)w-(1-\theta)(\sigma-\theta)\end{aligned}$$

The preceding wages Eq. (5.12) has no analytical solution for an arbitrary σ, but it offers much useful information. From (5.12), $w(\cdot)$ is well defined, which demonstrates how the wages' rate depends on trade integration. By using the implicit function theorem, we know that

$$w(0) = w(1) = 1,\ w'(0) = \frac{2\theta-1}{\theta(1-\theta)}\sigma > 0,\ w'(1) = -\frac{2\theta-1}{\sigma-1} < 0.$$

Moreover, Eq. (5.12) is a quadratic function of T. Therefore, for a given w, there are, at most, two roots of T that satisfy the wages equation. These properties imply that $w(T)$ has an inverted u-shape when T rises from 0 to 1. Furthermore, $w(T) > 1$ holds for all $T \in (0,1)$. When θ and σ are given a certain value ($\theta = 0.7$ and $\sigma = 3$), a simulation example of $w(T)$ can be plotted in the following (Fig. 5.1). the figure reveals some important features of wages in the large region. First, $w^* > 1$ holds for all $T \in (0,1)$. Moreover, equilibrium wages' rates have an inverted U-shape in T.

Equation (5.10) tells us that wages and HME in terms of firm share are equivalent.[2] This means that HME in terms of wages and firm share can be observed simultaneously. Since capital and labor are both employed as input, mobile capital makes firm in the larger region concentrate and brings them higher wages. Intuitively, more firms concentrated in the larger region can save transport costs, which also lead to a higher wages. More importantly, a non-monotonic relationship between wages and transport costs can be observed. The intuition that a region a higher concentration in a region increases wages implies that there are two opposing forces in the model. An increase in demand due to higher income encourages agglomeration. Simultaneously, higher wages increase labor costs for a firm, which encourages it relocate to some other region. However, this non-monotonic pattern in terms of wages and transport costs is seldom investigated in the related empirics.

[2]It is noteworthy that, despite the close relationship between $k_i(T)$ (firm share) and $w_i(T)$ (wages) shown in (10), $k_i(T)$ has a more complicated pattern when it is considered in multiregional situations. Uchikawa and Zeng (2014) investigate the relation between firm share and transport costs in a multiregional space and find that the $k_i(T)$ presents a more complicated pattern response to T. This result implies that we have to be prudent when testing HME in multiple regions. It seems reasonable to choose to empirically investigate the U-pattern in terms of wages other than firm share.

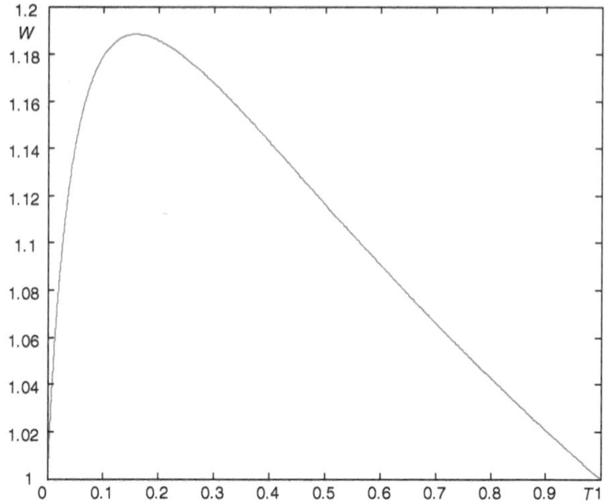

Fig. 5.1 Inverted U-shape between w^* and $T(\theta = 0.7$ and $\sigma = 3)$ *Source* Plotted by author on the basis of Eq. (5.12)

Through analysis of the theoretical framework, some interesting results can be obtained by a model with mobile capital as the production factor but without an agricultural sector. Since region j is assumed as the numéraire, i.e., $w_j = 1$, then $w^* > 1$ means $w_i > w_j$. This article indicates that the equilibrium wage in the larger region i exceeds the wages in the smaller region j due to market size asymmetries. This finding is also called the primary magnification effect (PME). Additionally, the forgoing analysis of $w(T)$ and Fig. 5.1 show that equilibrium wages' rates have an inverted U-shape in T. This implies that, with any increase in trade freeness, the relative wages between regions i and j experience a process from rising to falling. As argued by Head and Mayer (2004), to avoid confusion with PME, this is called the SME. PME implies that the wage disparity occurs between the two regions, but SME indicates that this inequality initially increase and then decreases during regional integration. above all, it is clarified in the present paper that HME carries two implications, namely the primary magnification effect and the SME. PME claims that the presence of a spatial wage disparity and SME demonstrates the trend of wage inequality when trade is more liberalized.

Before implementing the empirical part, several points should be mentioned. Compared with Behrens et al. (2009), although multiple regions are considered in their model, it also uses the agricultural sector and costless goods. Since labor is the only input of the agricultural sector, the factor prices are equalized. In this way, HME in terms of wages is not amenable to observation. The free-trade agricultural good helps to simplify the general equilibrium analysis, but it is also criticized by some scholars (e.g. Davis 1998). With only the manufacturing sector and transport costs, HME in terms of both firm share and wages can be observed in the theoretical model. More importantly, it should be noted that SME is always ignored in the related literature. If we consider HME as a magnification effect, it is closely related to trade costs. Furthermore, SME does not always bring about a positive effect. With further decreases in transport costs, a non-monotonic relationship is created.

As an exogenous variable, only a change in transport cost eventually leads to the magnification effect. SME could be considered the core element of HME. Moreover, a non-monotonic pattern of spatial inequality can be considered as a twinborn result to core-periphery model. Taken together, our empirical strategy consists of two main components. First of all, some stylized facts employing data from China are given to demonstrate the primary magnification effect of HME. Then the non-monotonic pattern of SME in terms of wages is empirically reinvestigated.

5.3 Primary Magnification Effect of HME

Head and Mayer (2004) clarify that, when taking the partial derivative of firm share (k) with respect to θ, $dk/d\theta > 1$ means the primary magnification effect, and it can be formulated as the definition of HME. This requires us prudently to define the magnification effect as a continuous function between firm share (k) and local demand (θ). As argued in Zeng (2014), $dk/d\theta > 1$ is limited to some specific assumptions and it is neither a necessary nor a sufficient condition for $k > \theta$ to hold. In line with our theoretical framework, the magnification of HME may simply be understood as the wages (or firm share) in larger region being higher than in the small region. It can also explained as follows: for any $T \in (0, 1)$, if $\theta_i > \theta_j$, then $w_i > w_j$. In addition, as discussed in the foregoing section, since SME in terms of firm share presents a more complex pattern than an inverted U-shape curve, we focus on investigating wages disparity to verify the primary magnification effect of HME. In this section, some data from China will be employed to clarify the facts of the primary magnification effect in terms of wages inequality.

Over the past three decades, China has become one of the world's fastest-growing economies by means of various reforms and its economic liberalization. However, alongside the economic development, China's transition to a market-oriented economy has created some new challenges, among which is the regional disparity between coastal and interior regions. This disparity has aroused much concern and social unrest. To date, most research in terms of regional inequality has concentrated on the macro level in terms of GDP or national income. While some studies compare the agglomeration of manufacturing or population, few efforts have been made to study the disparity in terms of wages between the coast and the interior, specifically in the field of wages for urban units. Further, most studies focus on a limited period, but this chapter prefers to investigate the long-term features and trend of spatial disparity in terms of wages between the coastal and interior regions of China.

We re-arrange all the provinces in China into two main parts, the larger coastal ones and the smaller interior one in line with a scale of the number of employed persons in urban units. To further reveal the difference within the interior regions, the interior is further divided into central and western parts according the criteria of

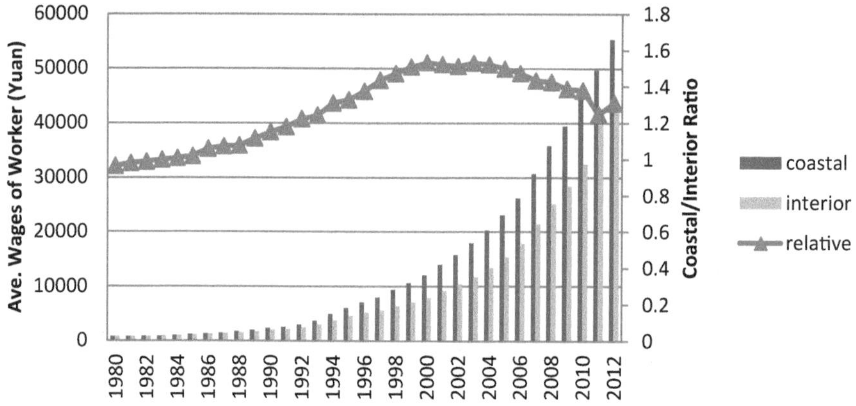

Fig. 5.2 Spatial wages disparity in China 1980–2012

China's National Bureau of Statistics.[3] The trend of coast-interior disparity in terms of the average wages of workers and staff in urban units is demonstrated in Fig. 5.2. From Fig. 5.2, we find that both coastal and interior provinces experienced rapid growth after the reform and opening up of the economy in terms of the average wages of workers and staff in urban units. However, the larger coastal area grew much faster than the interior. As a consequence, the inequality between the coast and the interior steadily increased during this period. Specifically, the wages rates showed that during the 1990s and early years of the 2000s, the increase in the disparity accelerated and then gradually stabilized. The definition of HME tells us that, other things being equal, wages are higher in a large region. According to the curve of the wages ratio between the coastal and interior regions shown in Fig. 5.2, the curve is consistently located above 1. This means that, in terms of the division based on the scale of the number of employed persons in urban units, the wages in the larger coastal region is always higher than in the smaller interior region. This finding also illustrates that the magnification effect could be observed throughout the regional integration during the study period. Moreover, the curve of the wages ratio shows that the trend of relative wages no longer presents a monotonic pattern. When regions are more integrated, a non-monotonic curve of wages inequality between the coast and the interior emerges. This magnification effect is strictly related to the freedom of trade between the coastal and interior regions. To avoid confusion with the primary magnification effect, it is called the SME.

[3]The two main regions defined in this chapter are the coastal ones and the interior ones. The coastal region consists of Liaoning, Beijing, Tianjin, Hebei, Shandong, Jiangsu, Shanghai, Zhejiang, Fujian and Guangdong); the interior consists of the central provinces (Shanxi, Anhui, Jiangxi, Hunan, Henan, Hubei, Heilongjiang, Jilin) and those in the west (Gansu, Qinghai, Ningxia, Xinjiang, Inner Mongolia, Guangxi, Sichuan, Chongqing, Guizhou, Yunnan, and Shaanxi). We have excluded Xizang and Hainan from the western and coastal regions respectively, due to lack of data.

5.4 SME and the Inverted U-Shaped Curve

5.4.1 Empirical Specification

It was demonstrated in the foregoing arguments that wages in large regions are higher than in small regions. But this primary magnification effect changes as trade freedom increases (the Secondary Magnification effect, SME). According to the results of theoretical model, we find that the relative wages between large regions and small regions initially increase and then decrease in T. This means that the relationship between the spatial wages' disparity and regional integration is not monotonic, and the inverted U-shaped curve holds. The empirical specification of SME is taken from analytical equilibrium condition of theoretical results. Then we can derive the following quadratic estimating equation to verify SME:

$$\frac{w_{it}}{w_{jt}} = \beta_0 + \beta_1 T_{ijt} + \beta_2 T_{ijt}^2 + \beta CV_{ijt} + \gamma_{ijt} \tag{5.13}$$

where w_{it}/w_{jt} is relative wages between the larger region i and small region j in year t, T_{ijt} is trade freedom between region i and region j in year t, and CV_{ijt} are controls for other things. T_{ijt} can also be understood as the level of regional integration between the two regions. If $\beta_1 > 0$ and $\beta_2 < 0$ by empirical analysis, this means that relative wages between larger and smaller regions evolve in an inverted U-shape during regional integration.

5.4.2 Data and Measurements

Our empirical study, using data from China, aims at evaluating the impacts of the increase of regional integration on the change in relative wages between the coastal and interior regions during the period 1980–2012. As in the primary magnification effect, we take each of the provinces in China as the geographic unit of analysis. In line with the scale of employed persons in urban units, we divide the 29 provinces into two groups, the coast and the interior. Since our empirical study aims to investigate the inverted U-shape of spatial wages inequality during regional integration within a home country, we consider two typical regions, one from the coastal provinces and the other from the interior provinces, as a pair for the spatial unit. Every two regions are matched to the point where the sample size is great enough to examine the change of spatial wages inequality during the increase of trade freedom. Relative wages w_{it}/w_{jt} as the dependent variable are computed by the ratio of the average wages of workers and staff in urban units in the coastal provinces to those in the interior provinces.

Transport costs as a key element of spatial economics, broadly speaking, encompass distance and trade barriers, time and energy. It is well known that there is no perfect method of measuring them. In the related empirical studies (Redding and Venables 2004; Ma 2006), distances are the main proxies for measuring transport costs, for international trade in particular. As mentioned by Combes and Lafourcade (2005), great circle distance or real time limit the possibility of applying them in a time series analysis. Geographers and transport planners have already developed advanced and accurate methodology with which to calculate transport costs by using real travel time, freight costs, or distance based on the Geographic Information System. Due to the scarcity of data sources, we here consider infrastructure, distance and road networks as representative of transport costs.

In our empirical analysis, we construct a new way to measure the transport costs by considering the distance as well as the level of infrastructure. One of the most obvious and powerful tools for representing the infrastructure level is a country's highway and railway networks. Inspired by Zheng (2010), this book uses the density of transport networks as a proxy to present accessibility in terms of regional trade. The density of transport costs within province p, which connects provinces i and j, is defined as follows:

$$Den_p^{ijt} = \frac{\mu_{ht} hl_{pt} + \mu_{rt} rl_{pt}}{Area_{pt}} \tag{5.14}$$

where hl_{pt} and rl_{it} are the total length of highway and railways in operation within a province at time t, and $Area_{pt}$ is the provincial territory of province p in year t. μ_{ht} and μ_{rt} are the weight of highways and railroads in the total freight volume in year t. The data on the infrastructure are from the National Bureau of Statistics of China and China's transportation statistical yearbook.

Furthermore, trade freeness between two provinces is represented. Each province can be considered as a node, and the trade freeness between the provinces i and j at year t is given by

$$T_{ijt} = \frac{1}{n^{ij}} \left(\sum_{p=1}^{n^{ij}} Den_p^{ijt} \right), \quad n^{ij} \geq 2 \tag{5.15}$$

Equation (5.14) measures how easily people and firms can interact with each other within a province. In addition, the trade freeness T_{ijt}, between region i and j, is defined as an arithmetical mean of the density from the starting region i and regions going through to the terminal region j. In China, the density of transport networks gets less from coastal regions to interior regions. In this book, a pair of provinces (one from the coastal and the other from interior) is selected as an individual in our sample, the provinces connecting the starting and terminal province are all from the interior. When a pair of provinces going through more provinces, it means that arithmetic mean of density will becomes less with the increase in n^{ij}, because more provinces with lower density of transport networks in the interior are included in

Eq.(5.15). Arithmetic mean of density is employed in measuring trade freeness, but it reflects the nature of trade freeness from the coastal to the interior in the case of China.

T_{ijt} measures the trade freeness between two regions, which can be explained as follows: A pair of provinces is selected as an individual in our sample, where the trade freeness is determined by two components, namely the distance between the starting region and the terminal one and the infrastructure level of every province. When we compare the trade freeness of any two pairs within the cross-sectional data, a pair going through more provinces indicates that trade freeness. If, for instance, we attempt to compare the trade freeness between Shanghai-Anhui and Shanghai-Sichuan in the same year, the trade freeness of the former pair is higher than the latter, because the latter goes through more provinces. In contrast, if we measure a pair of regions in the panel data with the constant distance between two provinces, trade freeness varies with the level of infrastructure. Over the last decade, the Chinese government has been investing a considerable amount on both the construction and maintenance of transportation networks. With the improved infrastructure, the increase in density indicates that trade is more integrated, and the trade freeness becomes higher. According to the theoretical model, the relationship between trade and transport costs is described as $T = \tau^{1-\sigma}$. Since $\sigma > 1$, larger trade freeness corresponds to smaller transport costs and $T \in (0, 1)$.

In this book, we focus on investigating the impact of trade integration on spatial wage disparity, but it is necessary to control for other related determinants of wage inequality. Since development disequilibrium is the feature of China's current economy, productivity and difference in education levels are important factors affecting wages across regions and should also be introduced in our estimation. The mean and standard deviation of these variables are shown in Table 5.1.

5.4.3 Empirical Results

A series of preliminary estimates obtained from regressing Eq. (5.13) are shown in Table 5.2. Columns 1, 4 and 7 are Feasible General Least Squares (FGLS) regression on trade freedom T and T^2 derived from data on the Coastal-Interior, Coastal-Central and Coastal-West, respectively. In order to better investigate regional integration on regional inequality, trade freedom alone is considered in the benchmark results.

We are first very concerned to find whether an increase of trade freedom does indeed affect regional inequality in wages due to SME. It is obvious that the coefficient for T is significantly positive at the 1% statistical level, and T^2, as we expected, is also significantly negative at the 1% statistical level. In Table 5.2 column 1, the coefficient of T is 3.607 and the T^2 coefficient is −3.91. When we look at T's quadratic model, we know from calculation that when T is over 0.461, there will be a decline of relative wages with every increase of trade freedom. In

Table 5.1 Definitions and statistics of variables

Variable	Definition	Mean	Std. Dev.	Min	Max
w_{it}/w_{jt}	Relative wages between region *i* and region *j*	1.295	0.400	0.553	2.754
T_{ijt}	Trade freeness, represented by the arithmetical mean of density from the starting region *i* and regions going through to the terminal region *j*	0.241	0.171	0.067	0.894
T_{ijt}^2	Square of T_{ijt}	0.087	0.131	0.005	0.800
Gp_i/Gp_j	Relative of GDP per capita between region *i* and region *j*	2.530	1.451	0.501	12.442
Hp_i/Hp_j	Relative number of students enrolled in regular institutions of higher education between region *i* and those enrolled in region *j*	6.132	6.088	0.340	43.342

Source National Bureau of Statistics of China and China's Transportation Statistical Yearbook

line with the definition of trade freeness in this book, the value of T is located in the interval of $(0, 1)$, when $T \in (0,\ 0.461)$, relative wages between coastal and interior regions increase in T, while when $T \in (0.461,\ 1)$, relative wages decrease in T.

To test the robustness of the results in different samples, FGLS estimations with both fixed effect (FE) and random effect (RE) are also used and shown in each group in Table 5.2. These empirical results indicate that the signs of T and T^2 are all compatible with our theoretical model, which supports the theoretical predictions regarding the inverted U-shape of relative wages during regional integration. It confirms that the relative wages between larger coastal regions and smaller interior regions initially increase and then decrease when T increases. After 1980, China's open economic policy was initially adopted in the coastal regions, and the central and western regions were influenced in turn. The improvement of infrastructure conditions between the coastal and interior regions, greater than the share of manufacturing firms located in coastal areas, also raised wages in the coastal provinces. However, in the long run, with sustainable development and further regional economic integration within China, the inequality in wages between the coastal and interior areas has gradually fallen. It is also consistent with these findings to find a non-linear relationship between regional inequalities and national development in the United States (Williamson 1965) and bell-shaped spatial inequality in the European Union (Barrios and Strobl 2009). Furthermore, the investigation of subunits in the interior, the Coastal-Central and Coastal-West areas, also supports the inverted U-pattern in terms of relative wages.

FGLS rather than OLS should be used, otherwise autocorrelation and heteroskedasticity may bias the estimates. Diagnostic tests of heteroskedasticity and autocorrelation were undertaken in the panel data of the analysis of the three groups in Table 5.2. The Breusch-Pagan/Cook-Weisberg test was employed for heteroskedasticity with $H_0 : \text{var}\ (\varepsilon^2) = \sigma^2 < \infty$. The Wooldridge test was used to test for autocorrelation with H_0: no first-order autocorrelation was found. Since both diagnostic test statistics are significant, AR (1) or heteroskedasticity exists

Table 5.2 Preliminary Results:1980–2012

	Full Sample			Coastal-Central			Coastal-West		
	FGLS	FE	RE	FGLS	FE	RE	FGLS	FE	RE
Dependent var. = w_i/w_j relative wages between coastal and interior regions									
$\boldsymbol{T}_{ij}$	3.607*** (29.56)	3.190*** (35.17)	3.204*** (35.28)	4.245*** (21.15)	3.934*** (26.35)	3.946*** (26.36)	3.562*** (20.34)	3.388*** (26.34)	3.388*** (26.30)
$\boldsymbol{T}_{ij}^2$	−3.91*** (24.47)	−3.640*** (30.77)	−3.647** (30.79)	−4.553*** (18.79)	−4.326*** (23.94)	−4.335** (23.93)	−4.155*** (16.22)	−4.299*** (22.81)	-1 −4.281*** (22.69)
Constant	0.763*** (45.25)	0.841*** (67.29)	0.838*** (38.81)	0.700*** (23.33)	0.760*** (34.33)	0.758*** (22.32)	0.759*** (34.75)	0.808*** (50.57)	0.809*** (28.65)
Obs	6110	6110	6110	2640	2640	2640	3470	3470	3470
Wald x^2	1258.52	748.64	1518.11	559.04	406.63	816.29	668.79	426.14	859.68
Year effect	Yes	Yes	Yes	Yes	Yes	Yes	Yes	Yes	Yes
Region effect	Yes	Yes	Yes	Yes	Yes	Yes	Yes	Yes	Yes
Diagnostic tests									
Breusch-Pagan/Cook-Weisberg test	929.04 [0.00]			415.88 [0.00]			473.19 [0.00]		
Wooldridge test	186.911 [0.00]			155.335 [0.00]			88.101 [0.00]		
Hausman test		76.74 [0.0012]			4.43 [0.795]			129.52 [0.000]	

Note Z-statistics in FGLS are given in parentheses. Figures in square brackets are *p*-values. The Breusch-Pagan/ Cook-Weisberg statistics provide a test for heteroskedasticity error structure, distributed as chi-square under the null of no heteroskedasticity across panels. The Wooldridge statistics provide a test for autocorrelation in panel data (H_0: no first-order autocorrelation), distributed as F under the null of no first-order autocorrelation. Time and country dummies were included in the estimation but for brevity their coefficients are not presented here

* denotes significance at 10% level

** denotes significance at 5% level

*** denotes significance at 1% level

within the panels, adopting the adjusted estimator in Table 5.2 corrected for heteroskedasticity and autocorrelation. In the Coastal-Interior and Coastal-West analysis in Table 5.2, the null hypothesis of Hausman tests was rejected, indicating that the fixed effects were consistent and efficient. In the 'Coastal-Central' group, however, the random effect was more consistent and efficient. However, the coefficients of both FE and RE in all groups are very similar.

In order to check the impact of productivity and education level difference between regions on relative wages, two control variables Gp_i/Gp_j and Hp_i/Hp_j were introduced in our estimations. Similar to Table 5.2, robustness tests were also used for comparison. The results shown in Table 5.3 reveal that even when considering other elements, the coefficients of T and T^2 are also significant at 1% and the signs are consistent with expectation. According to the FE results of column 3 in Table 5.3, we know that when T is over 0.439; there will be a decline of relative wages with every increase of trade freedom. This turning point is almost equal to the preliminary in Table 5.2. Moreover, we find that Table 5.3 shows that the coefficients of Gp_i/Gp_j and Hp_i/Hp_j are significant at the 1 percent level in the full sample group, indicating that relative wages were positively affected when the productivity of the eastern regions outstripped that of the interior. The FGLS (1) in Table 5.3 shows that when relative productivity between coastal and interior regions increases by 10%, then relative wages will rise by 1.3%. Similarly, when the density of higher education increases in the coastal regions, relative wages are significantly and positively affected. However, when the high density of education in the population was considered, the impact on relative wages of the productivity differentiation grew slightly less.

In FGLS (2) in Table 5.3, we observe that when Hp_i/Hp_j increase by 10%, relative wages increase by 0.13%. Meanwhile, the impact of productivity on wages changed from 0.13 in FGLS (1) to 0.104. This clarifies the case of China: The higher concentration of workers who have received higher education corresponds to the higher relative wages in this region. After controlling for autocorrelation and heteroskedasticity in the FGLS estimation, the coefficients of Gp_i/Gp_j and Hp_i/Hp_j become slightly higher than those in FE and RE estimates. In order to judge the impact of both control variables in different regions, we made two more sample tests in Table 5.4.

In Table 5.4, the coefficients of T^2 in terms of the 'Coastal-West' area became insignificant when the control variables were added, but the RE and FE results were still all significant, implying that the inverted U-shape in terms of the relative wages in the 'Coastal-West' area were not as stable as those of the full sample and the 'Coastal-Central' area. Comparing the results of this group with the group from the 'Coastal-West' area, the results of the 'Coastal-Central' are significant at 1%, even bearing in mind the control variables. The reason for this difference between central and west may be that the central regions are much nearer to the coastal area and these regions are more integrated. As for the influence of relative productivity, when the control variables are considered, it seems that the magnitude of coefficient of relative productivity become larger in FGLS (1) in Table 5.4, indicating that the

Table 5.3 Full Sample Tests in the coastal and interior regions:1980–2012

	FGLS (1)	FGLS (2)	FE	RE
Dependent var. = w_i/w_j *relative wages between the coastal and interior regions*				
$\boldsymbol{T_{ij}}$	2.887*** (27.32)	2.492*** (23.63)	2.917*** (30.05)	2.726*** (28.40)
$\boldsymbol{T^2_{ij}}$	−3.032*** (21.95)	−2.708*** (19.91)	−3.320*** (26.48)	−3.062*** (24.74)
$\boldsymbol{Gp_i/Gp_j}$	0.130*** (47.03)	0.104*** (33.48)	0.034*** (5.46)	0.068*** (13.18)
$\boldsymbol{Hp_i/Hp_j}$		0.013*** (17.41)	0.004*** (5.87)	0.006*** (8.25)
Constant	0.529*** (34.64)	0.578*** (38.05)	0.761*** (42.79)	0.685*** (34.70)
Obs	6048	6048	6048	6048
Wald x^2	3952.93	4383.65	399.92	1849.09
Year effect	Yes	Yes	Yes	Yes
Region effect	Yes	Yes	Yes	Yes
Diagnostic tests				
Breusch-Pagan/ Cook-Weisberg test	1541.58 [0.00]	1250.97 [0.00]		
Wooldridge test	184.520 [0.00]	182.282 [0.00]		
Hausman test			134.17 [0.00]	

Note Z-statistics in FGLS are given in parentheses. Figures in square brackets are *p*-values. The Breusch-Pagan/Cook-Weisberg statistics furnish a test for heteroskedasticity error structure, distributed as chi-square under the null of no heteroskedasticity across panels. The Wooldridge statistics provide a test for autocorrelation in panel data (H_0: no first-order autocorrelation), distributed as F under the null of no first-order autocorrelation. Time and country dummies were included in the estimation but for brevity their coefficients are not presented here

*denotes significance at 10% level

**denotes significance at 5% level

***denotes significance at 1% level

productivity difference has played a more important role in wage differentiation in Coastal-Central' area.

Most significantly, we confirm that there was SME after checking the trade freedom and relative wages of the coastal and interior regions as well as of the coastal-central and coastal-west areas in the period 1980–2012. The analysis has also shown the impact of economic determinants on relative wages: the coastal regions of China attracted more well-educated workers after 1980 and most manufacturing production focused on these regions, which increased the relative wages there and also led to higher standards of living in the coastal region of China than in the central and western regions.

Table 5.4 Robustness Tests in the 'Coast–Central' and 'Coast–West' groups:1980–2012

	Coastal-Central				Coastal-West			
	FGLS (1)	FGLS (2)	FE	RE	FGLS(3)	FGLS(4)	FE	RE
Dependent var. = w_i/w_j relative wages between coastal and interior regions								
$\boldsymbol{T_{ij}}$	3.281*** (19.51)	2.865*** (17.17)	3.920*** (23.89)	3.335*** (22.57)	2.650*** (17.64)	2.278*** (15.24)	3.014*** (21.65)	2.764*** (20.17)
$\boldsymbol{T_{ij}^2}$	−3.483*** (17.19)	−3.137*** (15.78)	−4.379*** (22.12)	−3.662*** (18.94)	−2.950 (13.46)	−2.634 (12.21)	−3.772*** (18.55)	−3.386*** (16.98)
$\boldsymbol{Gp_i/Gp_j}$	0.169*** (35.31)	0.139*** (26.29)	0.029*** (2.44)	0.072*** (7.55)	0.122*** (37.12)	0.099*** (26.51)	0.043*** (5.83)	0.070*** (11.37)
$\boldsymbol{Hp_i/Hp_j}$		0.013*** (12.45)	0.005*** (4.69)	0.008*** (7.22)		0.012*** (11.99)	0.004*** (3.71)	0.005*** (5.34)
Constant	0.455*** (17.68)	0.516*** (20.23)	0.803*** (27.17)	0.843*** (32.20)	0.541*** (27.93)	0.581*** (30.20)	0.708*** (32.08)	0.652*** (25.95)
Obs	2640	2640	2640	2640	3408	3408	3408	3408
Wald x^2	2041.36	2316.28	212.21	956.84	2524.21	2524.21	230.70	1066.20
Year effect	Yes	Yes	Yes	Yes	Yes	Yes	Yes	Yes
Region effect	Yes	Yes	Yes	Yes	Yes	Yes	Yes	Yes
Diagnostic tests								
Breusch-Pagan/ Cook-Weisberg test	1122.66 [0.00]	882.14 [0.00]			563.72 [0.00]	510.56 [0.00]		
Wooldridge test	164.146 [0.00]	156.585 [0.00]			86.725 [0.00]	84.504 [0.00]		
Hausman test			258.71 [0.00]				295.35 [0.00]	

Note Z-statistics in FGLS are given in parentheses. Figures in square brackets are *p*-values. The Breusch-Pagan/ Cook-Weisberg statistics furnish a test for heteroscedasticity error structure, distributed as chi-square under the null of no heteroscedasticity across panels. The Wooldridge statistics provide a test for autocorrelation in panel data (H_0: no first-order autocorrelation), distributed as F under the null of no first-order autocorrelation. Time and country dummies were included in the estimation but for brevity their coefficients are not presented here

*denotes significance at 10% level

**denotes significance at 5% level

***denotes significance at 1% level

5.5 Conclusion

To a large extent, spatial economics has come into the scope of mainstream economics. However, spatial economics still has some internal and external drawbacks and challenges, specifically in terms of empirical studies. As a key component of spatial economics, HME in terms of conception and empirical strategy is still under construction. It is argued that regional size affects the spatial configuration of economic activities, a phenomenon also known as HME. Within a theoretical framework based n Takahashi et al. (2013), the definition of HME is unpacked in our paper and is interpreted in terms of the wages in a larger region being higher than in a smaller one. It is noteworthy that this magnification also closely relates to the discrepancies in transport costs and relative wages between the larger and small regions, which evolve in a non-monotonic pattern when transport costs decline. To sum up, HME carries two implications, namely, the primary magnification effect and the secondary magnification effect.

This book empirically studied the HME in terms of wages in the case of China using panel data for the period 1980–2012. The finding suggested that wages in the larger coastal area are higher than in the interior due to the size difference between the regions. During regional integration, moreover, regional inequality in wages between the coastal and interior regions seemed to evolve in an inverted U-shape curve. This non-monotonic pattern was also verified by employing data between the 'Coast-West' and 'Coast-Central' areas in China. The evolution of space economics in China during the past three decades supports the inverted U-shaped pattern predicted by the theoretical models of spatial economics.

Employing data from an emerging country, China, this book investigated the existence of HME, specifically the bell-shaped pattern of wages. Consistent with Williamson (1965), and Barrios and Strobl (2009), regional inequality fluctuated over time. The empirical results from China indicated that the relative wages between the coastal and the interior regions initially increased and then decreased during regional integration. Our book can be viewed as an attempt to investigate the non-monotonic relationship between wages and trade freedom. Compared with the core-periphery pattern in spatial economics, economic re-dispersion or decentralization could be considered another typical phenomenon in practice. Due to the limited data sources, it is imperative to estimate the HME with data from different industries. The other revision that should be considered is the endogeneity issue, and some other reasonable controlling variables should be added.

Chapter 6
Conclusions

This book has investigated the industrial agglomeration and dispersion using NEG as the main framework. Since NEG has somewhat reached maturity in terms of conception and theory, especially in its two-region Dixit-Stiglitz-Iceberg form, at this moment, it is imperative for us to step back and inspect the models themselves. As Behrens et al. (2006a) claimed, the weakest point of the NEG model is geography itself. This book attempted to merge some elementary considerations such as first nature forces and economic mechanism to interpret the emerging industrial location patterns in developing nations. Particularly, this book extended the classic two-region core-periphery to a richer spatial scale and obtained the analytical results of this development. In detail, Chap. 1 explained the background and then proposed the main objective and organization of this book. Chapter 2 gave an introduction to the canonical NEG framework and reviewed the related literature. Then, Chap. 3 investigated the effects of international trade liberalization and integration of domestic regions on the space economy by considering full asymmetry in terms of regional size and trade accessibility. Chapter 4 analytically explained industrial agglomeration and dispersion by assuming that unskilled workers are employed both in the agricultural and manufacturing sectors. Chapter 5 further investigates the spatial disparity in terms of firm location and wage by taking account of one manufacturing sector and two production inputs. Even with CES utility function, the footloose capital model would bring some new findings. Moreover, evidence from China offers some verification that the home market effects in terms of spatial wage disparity presents an inverted U-shape pattern respect to regional integration.

Here, a conclusion and further discussion of these main five chapters will be provided.

J. Wang, *Economic Analysis of Industrial Agglomeration*,
https://doi.org/10.1007/978-981-10-7437-0_6

6.1 Summary of the Book

To better understand the background of this book, Chap. 1 first introduced the birth of new economic geography and analyzed the merits and drawbacks of spatial economics. It was shown that NEG provided rationales for the occurrence of economic agglomeration using a general equilibrium framework, but that it was still deficient in terms of several issues. Most NEG models overemphasized the role of pure economic mechanisms in explaining the formation of agglomeration, thereby neglecting geography. Moreover, although NEG models gave an explanation for the occurrence of agglomeration, these were largely unconcerned with where the agglomeration arose. Last, in related literature, industrial redispersion has received little attention. To settle this issue, the present book proposed the corresponding purposes and then introduced the organization of the book.

Chapter 2 presented a detailed overview of recent developments in NEG, which successfully applies the basic microeconomic principles to explain the endogenous formation of spatial agglomeration in the field of urban and regional economics. Then, a detailed explanation of Krugman's core-periphery model (1991) was provided. Additionally, subsequent refinements of the original C-P model, which mainly adopted a geographical viewpoint, were reviewed. It was pointed out that most of the existing NEG models are symmetrical in that regions or countries are assumed to have the same sizes and accessibilities to markets, which is not realistic and is unable to explain the real spatial economy. Chapter 2 concluded that it is important for NEG to take into account full asymmetry in terms of different regional sizes and accessibilities so that its theories can be adapted to more accurately reflect the real word.

In Chap. 3, this book extended Krugman's original NEG model to account for a two-country, three-region case where the home country was fully asymmetrical in terms of its size and access to global markets. The simulation results showed that the spatial economy of the home country changed in a more complex way than is shown in Krugman's results. When international trade liberalization continues but domestic regions remain poorly integrated, the gate region experiences a change from partial to full agglomeration. When the home country is closed to international trade, the decrease in domestic transport costs makes the hinterland more attractive for manufacturing. However, when it is open to global markets, more manufacturing is undertaken in the gate region.

The results obtained in Chap. 4 were able to explain both why and where industrial agglomeration and dispersion arise. The results also showed that when the international trade cost is very high, the space economy exhibits full agglomeration in the hinterland and then experiences a process of dispersion until an even industrial distribution exists between the two domestic regions. When the home country is open enough to world markets, firms will first concentrate in the hinterland and then gradually move to the gate region until a full agglomeration occurs during regional integration. With further regional economic integration, half of firms will again relocate to the hinterland, with the other half remaining in the gate region.

Chapter 5 went further. As in Krugman (1980, Sects. 1 and 2), the agricultural sector is moved away and there is only one sector that produces manufacturing varieties. Additionally, mobile capital as another production factor is also employed in addition to immobile labor. Since workers are immobile, a higher concentration of firms in a region results in increase of wages there. Final demand accordingly increases due to consumers' higher incomes, which is a centripetal force that encourages agglomeration. Simultaneously, a higher wage rate gives burden to the labor costs of firms, which is a centrifugal force that discourages agglomeration. When the regions are poorly integrated, centripetal forces are muted in the system, and firms prefer to serve the local market. In the other case, when the regions are highly integrated, centrifugal forces dominate in the system, dispersed location pattern emerges again. Deriving from Takahashi et al. (2013), it is clarified that wages in larger region are higher due to the advantage of market size and the wage rate also shows an inverted U-shape during the regional integration. Based on the theoretical framework, the empirical investigation is given by using panel data from China. The finding suggested that wages in the larger coastal area are higher than in the interior due to the size difference between the regions. During regional integration, moreover, regional inequality in wages between the coastal and interior regions seemed to evolve in an inverted U-shape curve. Employing data from an emerging country, China, this chapter investigated the existence of HME, specifically the bell-shaped pattern of wages predicted by the theoretical models of spatial economics.

6.2 Implications of the Book

This book first analyzed the impact of international trade liberalization and regional integration on the distribution of industrial activities within countries such as China. Full asymmetry in terms of transport accessibility and regional size was investigated, and some interesting and thought-provoking conclusions emerged. From this analysis, it has been demonstrated that economies of agglomeration occur from the interactions among economies of scale at the level of the individual producer, transport costs, and factor mobility. A clear understanding has also emerged of the tension between the centripetal and centrifugal forces. The simulation results were able to explain the success of coastal regions in China and the border regions of Mexico relative to other regions during international trade liberalization and regional integration. Although the simulation method had inherent defects, it was a good choice to investigate phenomena using a complex spatial scale, such as multi-region models.

The book was successful in giving an analytical result to explain industrial dispersion. Moreover, to better explain the reality of developing countries, it was assumed that unskilled workers are employed in both traditional and manufacturing sectors. This analysis suggested some further mechanisms related to why industrial redispersion emerged. It was demonstrated that the employment of unskilled workers in manufacturing firms constitutes another dispersive force that generates redispersion during economic integration. This allowed an interpretation of manufacturing firm relocation from core to periphery regions and the decrease in regional disparity in some emerging nations. What is more, the analytic results allow policy implications to be suggested in a way that is no longer tentative.

It has been more than two decades since the birth of new economic geography, but there seems to be an imbalance between the success of theoretical models and policy analysis. As discussed by Behrens and Robert-Nicoud (2011), NEG has almost nothing to say to policymakers, and the lack of sharp policy conclusions has led many researchers to refrain from prescribing any policy recommendations whatsoever. What makes the policy implication of NEG so hard? The investigation of models in this book identified the problem that the models of NEG have many properties that make the policy analysis very different from standard neoclassical models. The non-linearity, catastrophic changes, and multiple equilibriums all render the model vague when it comes to policy analysis. However, with the occurrence of a linear analytical model, NEG is easier to handle, yielding closed-form solutions to many questions. This also allows investigation of the relationship between trade costs (transport costs) and industrial location. Specifically, as Martin and Rogers (1995) pointed out, trade costs or transport costs could be interpreted as directly related to the quality of infrastructures. A reduction of transport costs can be regarded as an improvement in the domestic inter-regional infrastructure, while a drop in international trade costs represents the degree of integration of a country into global markets. For example, the construction of a highway between Shanghai and Chengdu (a core city in western China) will represent an improvement in infrastructure. The decrease in tariff or whether an open policy is adopted will relate to a drop in trade costs. The operability of trade (transport costs) makes NEG more energetic than it was before in terms of policy recommendations.

Based on the analytical results obtained in Chap. 4, the industrial agglomeration or dispersion within the home country is jointly determined by international trade costs and domestic transport costs. When the home country is open to world markets, with further decreases in transport costs, firms will relocate again and move from the agglomerated gate region to the hinterland. Eventually, an even distribution of firms between the two regions occurs. Fujita and Hu (2001) found that unequal development between the coastal region and hinterland is a major government concern. Hence, investment in the infrastructure between the gate region and hinterland could encourage their integration, such that manufacturing firms would relocate to the remote areas. The disparity between the core and periphery regions will be narrow. This also implies that government can give further support for infrastructure building to alleviate the overconcentration of industries in the center regions.

Compared with the core-periphery pattern in spatial economics, economic redispersion or decentralization could be considered as another typical phenomenon in practice. Being different from quasi-linear setting in Chap. 4, even with CES utility, the footloose capital model with only one manufacturing sector uncovers that HME contains two indispensable components PME and SME. Simultaneously, it is shown that HME in terms of firms share and wage are equivalent. The empirical section further verifies the existence of HME and wages in coastal regions are higher than those in the interior, due to the size differences between regions. Additionally, the evolution of the space-economy in China during the past three decades supports the inverted U-shape pattern predicted by the theoretical models of spatial economics. Regional disparity is a severe challenge to the central government of China after economic openness and reform. Based on the results in Chap. 5, the insight one can derive from the structural estimation is that further regional integration by virtue of improving infrastructure could alleviate spatial wage disparity.

6.3 Further Research Directions

This book has investigated a simple idea concerning how space economy evolves within a country during the regional integration and international trade liberalization. By utilizing the new economic geography framework, an economic model in which first nature and second nature were synthesized was created to analyze the economic spatial structure. Specifically, through an analytical model, industrial redispersion could be witnessed, giving insights into the phenomenon in the real world. Although the model used in this book was both simple and illuminating, a number of problems remain and future works should deal with these. The important directions for future works are given below.

(1) The identification of policy implications in this research was exciting and frustrating. It was exciting because studies on geographic economics are entering the mainstream and this work can offer a reasonable explanation for the formation of spatial disparity. On the other hand, it was frustrating because it is currently very difficult to obtain a precise idea of how regional policy would affect the spatial structure of the economy and what the associated productivity and welfare changes would be. The lack of sharp policy implications called for more work on this topic. Except the field that the tax competition is added into NEG (Baldwin and Krugman 2004; Kind et al. 2000; Ludema and Wooton 2000), it is unclear what future policy should look like. Further research is needed on this topic to proceed.
(2) Since early studies of NEG were all conducted according to the simulation method, there seems to be a paradox in terms of the promise of the theoretical model and the relative dearth of empirical work. Although the analytical part of this book can obtain the closed-form solution and investigate the evolution of the space economy within a country, it is still imperative to perform the related empirical studies in order to verify the theoretical conclusions. More specifically, numerical investigation done here could only provide a gallery of

possible equilibrium outcomes and relied heavily on a particular set of parameter values. We attempted to collect actual data from China to test the final results. More work will be required to design a good method to calculate the transport costs and trade costs and illuminate the asymmetrical considerations in this book.

(3) In this book, only workers were included as investment in the production function. In the simulation model, skilled workers were the only input representing the fixed and marginal costs of manufacturing; in the analytical model, both skilled and unskilled workers were considered to be production investments. However, we found that labor was internationally immobile and there was no investment mobility across countries in our model. In fact, the investment of capital for each differentiated good and the mobility of capital between countries, such as in foreign direct investment (FDI), are widespread in the real economy. Capital always seeks the highest-profit opportunities. Thus, more work will be required to consider both capital and labor as investment in production. These considerations will enable us to investigate the effects of globalization and industrialization on the industrial location.

(4) As Marshall (1920) claimed, external economies arise from (i) a pooled labor market; (ii) pecuniary externalities enabling the provision of non-traded inputs to an industry in a greater variety and at lower cost; and (iii) information or technological spillovers. In this book, the increasing returns, transport costs, demand linkage, and cost linkage created a circular logic agglomeration. This kind of mechanism is always considered to represent pecuniary externalities. The assumption that knowledge spills over was barely disputed. As a potential future direction, another important subject for NEG is how to bring knowledge spillovers into the economic model to analyze their impact across geographical space.

(5) In this book, two different utility functions i.e. constant elasticity of substitution (CES) and quasi-linear preferences are adopted in the theoretical framework. Nevertheless, the property of CES indicates that firm's profit-maximizing prices display constant markups over marginal costs. Due to its simplicity in calculation, CES is always employed in investigating monopolistic competition and increasing returns in a general equilibrium. However, a large amount of literature provides direct evidence that firm markups vary greatly across markets and industries (e.g. De Loecker 2011; De Loecker and Warzynski 2012; Feestra and Weinstem 2016; Lu et al. 2014). As argued in Chen and Zeng (2017), since international markets are substantially segmented, the so-called pricing-to-market is imperative to be incorporated in the models of spatial economics. In Chap. 4, quasi-linear utility function is used to analytically uncover the rationales of industrial agglomeration. Additionally, the endogenous markup can be obtained in with the framework of Ottaviano et al. (2002) and Melitz and Ottaviano (2008), which include a numéraire sector featured with perfect competition and linear technology. It implies that the wage will be equalized across regions. The income effects on price and agglomeration then become muted in quasi-linear models. Since the absence of income effects, quasi-linear framework is unable to observe

the facts that firm markups are higher in countries with higher per capital income in Simonovska (2015). As argued in Chen and Zeng (2017), a framework that features variable markups and that embeds income effects is encouraged. A tentative work by Chen and Zeng (2017) initiates a new framework which covers the income effects with variable elasticity of substitution (VES) preference. The role of VES can debunk the trade pattern, markups and firm location simultaneously in a global world with two factor production function. It is worth noting that even if VES is adopted in the theoretical framework, HME in terms of wage still occurs which further verifies the value of the empirical section in this book.

(6) NEG successfully opens the black box and endogenously uncovers the rationales of agglomeration. However, NEG in the past decades has focused on 'macro-heterogeneity' across locations indicating that how this can be endogenously generated by the microeconomic decisions of identical people and firms (Ottaviano 2011). The wave of heterogeneity initiated by Melitz (2003) has launched new—new trade theory(NNTT). As NEG originating from new trade theory, NEG could naturally evolve into a 'new' NEG (NNEG), with consideration of firm heterogeneity in productivity. Baldwin and Okubo (2006) show that when productivity differences across firms are incorporated together with differences between locations, the firm with low productivity will relocate to periphery to avoid fierce competition stemming from agglomeration. In the presence of heterogeneous agents, the allocation of firm or workers across regions becomes an interesting topic to explore. The spatial sorting and selection of heterogeneous agent poses significant impacts on composition, productivity and size of region.

References

Ago, T., Isono, I., & Tabuchi, T. (2006). Locational disadvantage of the hub. *Annals of Regional Science, 40,* 819–848.

Amiti, M., & Javorcik, B. S. (2008). Trade costs and the location of foreign firms in China. *Journal of Development Economics, 85,* 129–149.

Baldwin, R. E., & Krugman, P. R. (2004). Agglomeration, integration and tax harmonization. *European Economic Review, 48,* 1–23.

Baldwin, R., Forslid, R., Martin, P., Ottaviano, G., & Robert-Nicoud, F. (2003). *Economic geography and public policy*. Princeton University Press.

Baldwin, R., & Okubo, T. (2006). Heterogeneous firms, agglomeration and economic geography: Spatial selection and sorting. *Journal of Economic Geography, 6,* 323–346.

Barrios, S., & Strobl, E. (2009). The dynamics of regional inequalities. *Regional Science and Urban Economics, 39,* 575–591.

Behrens, K. (2011). International integration and regional inequalities: How important is national infrastructure. *The Manchester School, 79*(5), 952–971.

Behrens, K., & Gaigne, C. (2006). Developing the outermost regions of Europe: Some lessons from economic geography. Report prepared for the conference: La situation macroeconomique de l'ultraperipherir europeenne. Brussels, December 15, 2006.

Behrens, K., & Robert-Nicoud, F. (2009). Krugman's paper in regional science: the 100 dollar bill on the sidewalk is gone and the 2008 Nobel Prize well-deserved. *Paper in Regional Science, 88*(2), 467–490.

Behrens, K., & Robert-Nicoud, F. (2011). Tempora mutantur: In search of a new testament for NEG. *Journal of Economic Geography, 11*(2), 215–230.

Behrens, K., Gaigne, C., Ottaviano, G., & Thisse, J.-F. (2006). Is remoteness a locational disadvantage? *Journal of Economic Geography, 6,* 347–368.

Behrens, K., Gaigne, C., Ottaviano, G., & Thisse, J.-F. (2006). How density economies in international transportation link the internal geography of trading partners. *Journal of Urban Economics, 60,* 248–263.

Behrens, K., Gaigne, C., Ottaviano, G., & Thisse, J.-F. (2007). Countries, regions and trade: On the welfare impacts of economic integration. *European Economic Review, 51,* 1277–1301.

Behrens, K., Lamorgese, A., Ottaviano, G., & Tabuchi, T. (2009). Beyond the home market effect: Market size and specialization in a multi-country world. *Journal of International Economics, 79,* 259–265.

Chen, C., & Zeng, D.-Z. (2017). Mobile capital, variable elasticity of substitution, and trade liberalization. *Journal of Economic Geography* forthcoming.

Combes, P., & Lafourcade, M. (2005). Transport costs: Measures, determinants, and regional policy implications for France. *Journal of Economic Geography, 5,* 319–349.

Crozet, M., & Koenig, P. (2004). EU Enlargement and the Internal Geography of Countries. *Journal of Comparative Economics, 32,* 265–279.

J. Wang, *Economic Analysis of Industrial Agglomeration*,
https://doi.org/10.1007/978-981-10-7437-0

Davis, R. (1998). The home market, trade, and industrial structure. *American Economic Review, 88,* 1264–1276.

Davis, R., & Weinstein, E. (1999). Economic geography and regional production structure: An empirical investigation. *European Economic Review, 43*(2), 379–407.

Davis, R., & Weinstein, E. (2003). Market access, economic geography and comparative advantage: An empirical assessment. *Journal of International Economics, 59*(1), 1–23.

Deichmann, U., Kaiser, K., Lall, S., & Shalizi, Z. (2005). Agglomeration, transport and regional development in Indonesia. Policy Research Working Paper 3477. *World Bank, Washington, D. C.*

De Loecker, J. (2011). Product differentiation, multiproduct firms, and estimating the impact of trade liberalization on productivity. *Econometrica, 79*(5), 1407–1451.

De Loecker, J., & Warzynski, F. (2012). Markups and firm-level export status. *American Economic Review, 102*(6), 2437–2471.

Dixit, A. K., & Stiglitz, J. E. (1977). Monopolistic competition and optimal product diversity. *American Economic Review, 67,* 297–308.

Fan, C. C., & Sun, M. (2008). Regional inequality in China: 1978–2006. *Eurasian Geography and Economics, 49*(1), 1–20.

Fally, T., Paillacar, R., & Terra, C. (2010). Economic geography and wages in Brazil: Evidence from micro-data. *Journal of Development Economics, 91,* 155–168.

Feenstra, R. C., & Weinstein, D. E. (2016). Globalization, markups, and U.S. Welfare. *Journal of Political Economy, 125*(4), 1040–1074.

Forslid, R., & Ottaviano, G. T. (2003). An analytically solvable core-periphery model. *Journal of Economic Geography, 3,* 229–240.

Fujita, M., & Hu, D. (2001). Regional disparity in China 1985–1994: The effects of globalization and economic liberalization. *The Annals of Regional Science, 35,* 3–37.

Fujita, M., & Mori, T. (2005). Frontiers of the new economic geography. *Papers in Regional Science, 84,* 377–407.

Fujita, M., Krugman, P. R., & Venables, A. J. (1999). *The spatial economy: Cities, regions and international trade.* Cambridge, MA: MIT Press.

Gallup, J. L., Sachs, J. D., & Mellinger, A. (1999). Geography and economic development. *International Regional Science Review, 22,* 179–232.

Garretsen, H., & Martin, R. L. (2010). Rethinking (new) economic geography models: Taking geography and history more seriously. *Spatial Economic Analysis, 5,* 127–160.

Geyer, H. S., & Kontuly, T. M. (1996). *Differential urbanization: Integrating spatial models.* London:Arnold.

Golubchikov, Oleg. (2006). Interurban development and economic disparities in a Russian Province. *Eurasian Geography and Economics, 47*(4), 478–495.

Haddad, E. A., Domingues, E. P., & Perobelli, F. S. (2002). Regional effects of economic integration: The case of Brazil. *Journal of Policy Modeling, 24,* 453–482.

Haddad, E. A., & Perobelli, F. S. (2003a). Interdependence among the Brazilian States: An Input–Output approach, REAL *Discussion Paper* 03-T-18, University of Illinois at Urbana-Champaign.

Haddad, E. A., & Perobelli, F. S. (2003b). An exploratory spatial data analysis of Brazilian Interregional Trade (1985–1996), REAL *Discussion Paper* 03-T-22, University of Illinois at Urbana-Champaign.

Hanson, G. H. (1996). Agglomeration, dispersion, and the pioneer firm. *Journal of Urban Economics, 39,* 255–281.

Hanson, G. H. (2005). Market potential, increasing returns, and the geographic concentration. *Journal of International Economics, 67*(1), 1–24.

Head, K., & Mayer, T. (2004). The empirics of agglomeration and trade. In J. V. Henderson & J.-F. Thisse (Eds.), *Handbook of regional and urban economics* (Vol. 4). Amsterdam: North Holland.

Head, K., & Mayer, T. (2006). Regional wages and employment responses to market potential in the EU. *Regional Science and Urban Economics, 36*(5), 573–594.

Head, K., & Ries, J. (2001). Increasing returns versus national product differentiation as an explanation for the pattern of US–Canada trade. *American Economic Review, 91*(4), 858–876.

Helpman, E. (1998). The size of regions. In D. Pines, E. Sadka, & I. Zilcha (Eds.), *Topics in public economics: Theoretical and applied analysis* (pp. 33–54). Cambridge: Cambridge University Press.

Helpman, E., & Krugman, P. (1985). *Market structure and foreign trade: Increasing returns, imperfect competition, and the international economy*. Cambridge: MIT Press.

Henderson, J. V., Lee, T., & Lee, J.-Y. (2001). Scale externalities in Korea. *Journal of Urban Economics, 49,* 479–504.

Hering, L., & Poncet, S. (2010). Market access and individual wages: Evidence from China. *Review of Economic Statistics, 92*(1), 145–159.

Holmes, T. J., & Stevens, J. J. (2004). Spatial distribution of economic activities in North America. In J. V. Henderson & J.-F. Thisse (Eds.), *Handbook of regional and urban economics* (Vol. 4, pp. 2797–2843). Amsterdam: North-Holland.

Kind, H. J., Midelfart Knarvik, K. H., & Schjelderup, G. (2000). Competing for capital in a 'lumpy' world. *Journal of Public Economics, 78,* 253–274.

Krugman, P. (1980). Scale economies, product differentiation, and the pattern of trade. *American Economic Review, 70,* 950–959.

Krugman, P. R. (1991). Increasing returns and economic geography. *Journal of Political Economy, 99,* 483–499.

Krugman, P. R., & Venables, A. J. (1995). Globalization and inequality of nations. *Quarterly Journal of Economics, 110*(4), 857–880.

Krugman, P., & Livas Elizondo, R. (1996). Trade policy and the third world metropolis. *Journal of Development Economics, 49,* 137–150.

Krugman, P. (2011). The new economic geography, now middle-aged. *Regional Studies, 45,* 1–7.

Kwon, W.G . 1985. Issues and problems in Planning and Implementing Industrial Location Policy in Korea. Discussion paper, *World Bank*, Washington DC.

Lu, Y., Tao, Z., & Yu, L. (2014). The markup effect of agglomeration. Working Paper.

Ludeman, R. D., & Wooton, I. (2000). Economic geography and the fiscal effects of regional integration. *Journal of International Economics, 52,* 331–357.

Ma, A. C. (2006). Geographic location of foreign direct investment and wages inequality in China. *World Economy, 29*(8), 1031–1055.

Marshall, A. (1920). *Principles of economics*. London: Macmillan.

Martin, P., & Rogers, C. A. (1995). Industrial location and public infrastructure. *Journal of International Economics, 39,* 335–351.

Melitz, M. J. (2003). The impact of trade on intra-industry reallocations and aggregate industry productivity. *Econometrica, 71,* 1695–1725.

Melitz, M. J., & Ottaviano, G. I. P. (2008). Market size, trade, and productivity. *Review of Economic Studies, 75*(1), 295–316.

Monfort, P., & Nicolini, R. (2000). Regional convergence and international integration. *Journal of Urban Economics, 48,* 286–306.

Ottaviano, G. I. P., Tabuchi, T., & Thisse, J.-F. (2002). Agglomeration and trade revisited. *International Economic Review, 43,* 409–436.

Ottaviano, G. I. P. (2002). Models of 'new economic geography': factor mobility vs. vertical linkages. Mimeo, Graduate Institute of International Studies.

Ottaviano, G. I. P., & Thisse, J.-F. (2004). Agglomeration and economic geography. In J. V. Henderson & J.-F. Thisse (Eds.), *Handbook of regional and urban economics* (Vol. 4, pp. 2563–2608)., Cities and Geography Amsterdam: North-Holland.

Ottaviano, G. I. P. (2011). 'New' new economic geography: Firm heterogeneity and agglomeration economies. *Journal of Economic Geography, 11*(2), 231–240.

Paluzie, E. (2001). Trade policy and regional inequalities. *Papers in Regional Science, 80,* 67–85.

Picard, P., & Zeng, D.-Z. (2005). Agricultural sector and industrial agglomeration. *Journal of Development Economics, 77,* 75–106.
Picard, P. M., & Zeng, D.-Z. (2010). A harmonization of first and second natures. *Journal of Regional Science, 50,* 973–994.
Pflüger, M. (2004). A simple, analytically solvable, Chamberlinian agglomeration model. *Regional Science and Urban Economics, 34,* 565–573.
Pflüger, M., & Tabuchi, T. (2010). The size of regions with land use for production. *Regional Science and Urban Economics, 40*(6), 481–489.
Puga, D. (1999). The rise and fall of regional inequalities. *European Economic Review, 43,* 303–334.
Puga, D., & Venables, A. J. (1996). The spread of industry: Spatial agglomeration in economic development. *Journal of the Japanese and International Economies, 10,* 440–464.
Redding, S. J., & Venables, A. J. (2004). Economic geography and international inequality. *Journal of International Economics, 62*(1), 53–82.
Robert-Nicoud, F. (2002). *A simple geography model with linkages and capital mobility*. London School of Economics: Mimeo.
Robert-Nicoud, F. (2005). The structure of simple 'new economic geography' models (or, on identical twins). *Journal of Economic Geography, 5*(2), 201–234.
Simonovska, I. (2015). Income differences and prices of tradables: Insights from an online retailer. *Review of Economic Studies, 82*(4), 1612–1656.
Suedekum, J. (2006). Agglomeration and regional costs of living. *Journal of Regional Science, 46,* 529–534.
Tabuchi, T. (1998). Agglomeration and dispersion: A synthesis of Alonso and Krugman. *Journal of Urban Economics, 44,* 333–351.
Tabuchi, T., & Thisse, J.-F. (2002). Taste heterogeneity, labor mobility and economic geography. *Journal of Development Economics, 69,* 155–177.
Takahashi, T., Takatsuka, H., & Zeng, D.-Z. (2013). Spatial inequality, globalization, and footloose capital. *Economic Theory, 53,* 213–238.
Takatsuka, H., & Zeng, D.-Z. (2009). Dispersion forms: an interaction of market access, competition, and urban costs. *Journal of Regional Science, 49*(1), 177–204.
Venables, A. J. (1996). Equilibrium locations of vertically linked industries. *International Economic Review, 37,* 951–958.
Wang, J., & Xu, J.-Q. (2015). Home market effect, spatial wages disparity: An empirical reinvestigation of China. *Annals of Regional Science, 55,* 313–333.
Wang, J., & Zheng, X.-P. (2012). Developments of new economic geography: From symmetry to asymmetry. *Ritsumeikan Economic Review, 61*(2), 58–76.
Wang, J., & Zheng, X.-P. (2013). Industrial agglomeration: Asymmetry of regions and trade costs. *Review of Urban & Regional Development Studies, 25*(2), 61–78.
Wang, J., & Zheng, X.-P. (2013). Industrial agglomeration and dispersion in gate and Hinterland Region. *Ritsumeikan Economic Review, 62*(1), 39–60.
Williamson, J. G. (1965). Regional inequality and the process of national development. *Economic Development and Culture Change, 13,* 3–45.
Zeng, D.-Z. (2006). Redispersion is different from dispersion: spatial economy of multiple industries. *Annals of Regional Science, 40*(2), 229–247.
Zeng, D.-Z. (2014). The role of country size in spatial economics: A survey of the home market effects. *Proceedings of the Rijeka Faculty of Economics Journal of Economics and Business, 32*(2), 379–403.
Zeng, D.-Z., & Uchikawa, T. (2014). Ubiquitous inequality: The home market effect in a multicounty space. *Journal of Mathematical Economics, 50,* 225–233.
Zeng, D.-Z., & Zhao, L.-X. (2010). Globalization, interregional and international inequalities. *Journal of Urban Economics, 67,* 352–361.
Zheng, X.-P. (2010). A cointegration analysis of dynamics externalities. *Japan and World Economy, 22,* 130–140.

Kolibri 360 GmbH
Ferdinand-Jühlke-Straße 7
99095 Erfurt, Deutschland
produktsicherheit@kolibri360.de